STEVE
SHEINKIN

★ ★ ★

LINCOLN'S GRAVE ROBBERS

SCHOLASTIC
FOCUS

New York

Photo Research: Dwayne Howard

Photos ©: cover center and background: Abraham Lincoln Presidential Library and Museum; ii-iii: Meserve-Kunhardt Collection, Beinecke Rare Book & Manuscript Library, Yale University; iv-v: Andy Dean Photography/Shutterstock; vi top left and right: Abraham Lincoln Presidential Library and Museum; vii: I. Pilon/Shutterstock; viii: spxChrome/ iStockphoto; ix: Meserve-Kunhardt Collection, Beinecke Rare Book & Manuscript Library, Yale University; 5: The Granger Collection; 8: Courtesy of the Tyrrell Family; 10: The Print Collector/Alamy Stock Photo; 16: U.S. Department of the Treasury; 22, 24: United States Mint; 30: Library of Congress; 34: Abraham Lincoln Presidential Library and Museum; 38: Original art by Lloyd Ostendorf; 40: The Granger Collection; 45: Library of Congress; 47, 48: The Granger Collection; 50: Abraham Lincoln Presidential Library and Museum; 51, 53, 55: Library of Congress; 56, 58, 61: Abraham Lincoln Presidential Library and Museum; 64 left and right: The Granger Collection; 66, 69: Abraham Lincoln Presidential Library and Museum; 88: Ralph Crane/Getty Images; 90: Meserve-Kunhardt Collection, Beinecke Rare Book & Manuscript Library, Yale University; 108: Abraham Lincoln Presidential Library and Museum; 114: Library of Congress; 139: Meserve-Kunhardt Collection, Beinecke Rare Book & Manuscript Library, Yale University; 140: Courtesy Steve Sheinkin; 154: Meserve-Kunhardt Collection, Beinecke Rare Book & Manuscript Library, Yale University; 187: Abraham Lincoln Presidential Library and Museum; 193: Meserve-Kunhardt Collection, Beinecke Rare Book & Manuscript Library, Yale University; 195: Library of Congress; 196: Abraham Lincoln Presidential Library and Museum.

This book was originally published in hardcover by Scholastic Press in 2013.

ISBN 978-1-338-29013-4

10 9 8 7 6 5 4 3 2   19 20 21 22

Printed in the U.S.A. 23

This edition first printing 2018

Book design by Kay Petronio

For Sara
this is her kind of story

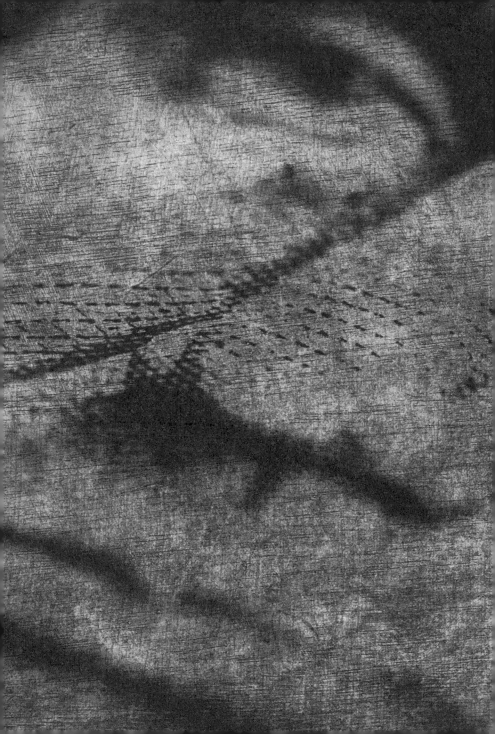

CONTENTS

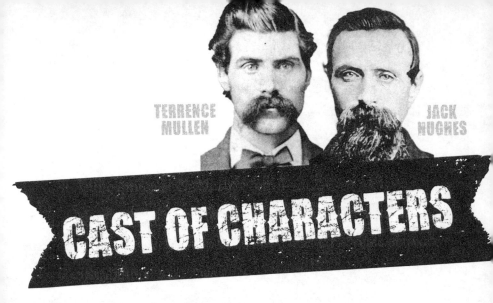

TERRENCE MULLEN

JACK HUGHES

CAST OF CHARACTERS

The Counterfeiters & Body Snatchers

Allie Boyd – counterfeiter, wife to Ben Boyd

Benjamin Boyd – one of the nation's top engravers of counterfeit plates

Mary Butterworth – skilled counterfeiter in early 1700s Massachusetts

Jack Hughes – shover of counterfeit currency, one of the Lincoln body snatchers

25

James "Big Jim" Kennally – boss of counterfeiting ring, mastermind behind Lincoln body snatching plot

Nat Kinsey – expert engraver, Secret Service informer

Pete McCartney – famous counterfeiter, brother-in-law to Ben Boyd

Terrence Mullen – distributor of counterfeit currency, one of the Lincoln body snatchers

Thomas Sharp – leader of counterfeiting gang, failed in first attempt to steal Lincoln's body

The Lawmen

James Brooks – chief of the Secret Service at time of body snatching plot

George Hay – private detective, hired by Tyrrell to catch body snatchers

John McDonald – Secret Service agent, worked for Tyrrell

John McGinn – private detective, hired by Tyrrell to catch body snatchers

Patrick Tyrrell – Chief Operative of Chicago District of the Secret Service, led attempt to catch body snatchers

Elmer Washburn – former chief of the Secret Service, assisted Tyrrell on body snatching case

Other Key Characters

Belle Bruce – resident of Springfield, helped expose first plot to steal Lincoln

Charles Deane – Chicago lawyer, friend of Patrick Tyrrell

John English – *Chicago Tribune* reporter, first to break story of attempted tomb robbery

Rutherford B. Hayes – Republican candidate for president in 1876

Mary Todd Lincoln – widow of Abraham Lincoln

Bill Neely (A.K.A. "Billy Brown") – Chicago bricklayer, roper for Secret Service

William O'Brien – defense lawyer, defended Hughes and Mullen at trial

John Carroll Power – custodian of Lincoln Monument

Samuel Tilden – Democratic candidate for president in 1876

Lewis C. Swegles – career criminal, roper who informed Secret Service of plot to steal Lincoln's body

Prologue

MIDNIGHT ESCAPE

A passenger train rattled through the woods of western Pennsylvania late one summer night in 1864. In the rear car sat a man with a black beard. Iron shackles and chains bound his wrists and ankles. Armed guards sat on either side of him.

The train was on its way to Washington, DC. Pete McCartney was headed for the dreaded Old Capitol Prison. Or so it appeared.

The prisoner turned and looked through the open door at the rear of the car. Judging by the speed the train slid past moonlit clumps of trees, he figured they were doing thirty-five miles an hour. A bit fast for what he needed to do.

He glanced at the guards, one seated beside him, another across the aisle. Each seemed lost in his own thoughts.

McCartney sprang up. He stumbled and slid on short steps, chains clanking, down the aisle and through the open door. The guards dashed onto the platform just in time to see the prisoner dive over the side and smack the gravel slope along the tracks—and disappear into the darkness.

One of the soldiers lunged for the alarm cord strung along the side of the car. The steam whistle on the roof let loose an earsplitting blast and the train began screeching to a stop.

"What is it?" asked a startled passenger.

"McCartney has escaped!" yelled one of the guards.

"And who is McCartney?"

"How has he escaped?"

"Gone out at the car door!" the guard shouted.

"When?"

"Now—this moment!"

"While the train was in motion?" asked a stunned conductor.

"Confound that fellow!" grunted one of the guards as he jumped from the slowing train.

"Well, he's smashed every bone in his skin, at all events," the other said as he jumped.

They hurried back along the dark tracks, swinging

lanterns, expecting to come quickly to the prisoner's mangled body. But there was no sign of him.

"I was hurt, of course," McCartney later said of his midnight leap. "But I fled to the woods, waited till all was quiet, and the train had gone, struggled along for hours, skulked and secreted myself, and with a stone finally smashed the iron shackles from my limbs."

McCartney was hungry, bruised as a rotting apple, and lost somewhere in the forest far from home. But he wasn't going to jail. And that's all that mattered.

This was far from his first escape.

Pete McCartney was a counterfeiter—a coney man, as government agents called them. He'd been arrested many times for making and passing fake money, but had always found ways to wriggle free. McCartney busted out of one prison by patiently collecting foil from the insides of tobacco packages, melting the metal with a candle, and molding it into a key to his jail cell. Usually his method of escape was a lot simpler: He bought his way out.

"I was always a cash man, you know," McCartney

bragged. "I have paid away over $70,000 first and last, in good money, to escape the clutches of the law." He wasn't sure he could bribe his way out of the Old Capitol Prison, which explains the dangerous train escape. "I was aware there was risk in jumping from the cars when the train was flying along at such a rate," he explained. "But then, we have to take risks as we meet with them."

After such a close call on the train, McCartney tried to go straight. He drifted back to his native Midwest and opened a photography studio. Then he moved to another town and bought a livery stable. Knowing the police were after him, he couldn't stay in one place. "I practiced dentistry for a while," he said, "but this was too slow for me." He even earned money as a traveling lecturer, giving talks on the art of detecting counterfeit currency.

But the lure of easy money was too strong—he started counterfeiting again. "I shoved a good many notes as I traveled," admitted McCartney. "The officers got on my trail." He was arrested in Cincinnati, escaped, was recaptured in Illinois and taken to jail in the state capital of Springfield.

Old Capitol Prison in Washington, DC

When the news reached Washington, DC, an excited Herman Whitley hopped on a train and headed west. An ex–Union Army officer, Whitley was now chief of the United States Secret Service, a new government agency in charge of battling counterfeiters. He knew all about Pete McCartney, and was eager to question him.

Whitley's interview with the coney man was a bit disappointing. McCartney offered to turn over his stash of bogus cash, but refused to squeal on other well-known counterfeiters.

The chief got up to leave.

"You won't leave me here, I suppose?" McCartney asked, seeming surprised.

"Yes, for the present," said Whitley. "You're safe here."

"Oh, I can get out of this place easy enough," McCartney said, grinning. "I have done so before, and I can do it again."

"I guess not," Whitley said.

"Where are you stopping, Colonel?"

Whitley mentioned the name of his hotel.

"Your number?"

"Room twenty-four."

"Thank you," said McCartney. "I will call on you, at ten."

Whitley smiled. He could enjoy a good joke, even from a crook. "Good night," he said.

At ten o'clock that night, Whitley was sitting at the desk in his hotel room, writing up a report. There was a gentle knock on the door.

"Come in," said the chief.

The door opened. A voice sang out, "Good evening, Colonel!"

Whitley turned to his guest. "McCartney!" he shouted, drawing his revolver. "How are you here?"

"Put up your shootin' iron, Colonel," McCartney said. "I merely called to pay my respects. I am going back, of course."

And McCartney really did walk back to prison. Smiling all the way.

Herman Whitley never did figure out how McCartney got out of jail that night. However he did it, the stunt illustrated a serious challenge facing the U.S. government in the 1870s. The Secret Service was absolutely *determined* to catch counterfeiters and keep them behind bars. But coney men were just as eager to get free— and they were good at it, too.

On a freezing morning in February 1875, Patrick Tyrrell hopped off a streetcar in downtown Chicago, Illinois. A massive fire had gutted the city just four years before, but Chicago was already roaring back to life. Stone buildings were rising all around, and the wide sidewalks were jammed with people in a hurry.

Tyrrell stepped through the doors of the newly rebuilt Palmer House hotel and stood in the cavernous lobby. With its shining marble, glittering chandeliers, and columns reaching up to soaring ceilings, the

Patrick Tyrrell

place looked more like an overgrown palace than a hotel. But Tyrrell wasn't here to admire the architecture. He asked a clerk for the room number of his boss, the new Secret Service chief Elmer Washburn.

A powerfully built man with thick black hair, Tyrrell had spent his adult life chasing down crooks as a Chicago detective. Now forty-four, he was one of the newest operatives of the United States Secret Service. He knew all about coney men like Pete McCartney. It was his job to put them out of business.

The operative found Washburn's room, and the two men sat down to talk. The subject was the usual one: counterfeiters, and how to nab them. Specifically, Washburn had taken the train from Washington to talk to Tyrrell about a particularly dangerous coney man, an expert engraver, and brother-in-law to Pete McCartney. The man was an even bigger thorn in the government's side than McCartney. In fact, he was a threat to the nation's entire economic system.

His name was Benjamin Boyd.

Born in Cincinnati in 1834, Boyd was the son of a master

A street scene in Chicago during the late 1800s

engraver—engravers cut designs and pictures into metal plates, and the plates were then used to make prints on paper. Young Ben showed interest in his father's craft, and obvious artistic talent. When Ben was still a teenager, his father set him up to study with one of the city's best engravers. The plan was that one day Ben would take over the family business.

Other Cincinnati engravers noticed Boyd's skill, and one of them, Nat Kinsey, offered to teach the kid a few advanced techniques. Kinsey was known for his beautifully intricate engravings of landscapes. It was less well known that with that same steady hand and attention to detail, he also cut plates to print counterfeit money.

Ben was tempted by the idea of making money—literally *making* it. And he learned quickly from Kinsey. At the age of twenty, hunched over the desk in his room at his father's house, he cut his first two counterfeit plates: the front and back of a $20 bill.

The quality of this twenty was Boyd's ticket into the secret world of counterfeiting. He hopped around the Midwest, cutting plates and printing "coney." Distributors bought the goods from him, usually for at least 15 percent of the fake money's face value. Distributors then doubled the price and sold the bills to "shovers," whose job it was to pass the counterfeit cash in stores and banks.

The potential profits were enormous. From just one set of $50 plates, Boyd printed $265,000—about $6 million in today's money! But it was a risky way to get rich. Boyd was arrested in Iowa in 1859, and sentenced to two years in the state penitentiary.

After his release, Boyd moved to Illinois and went right back to cutting counterfeit plates. He partnered with Pete McCartney and they set up a workshop in Mattoon.

At some point in the early 1860s, Boyd met a young woman named Almiranda Ackman, a pretty brunette, according to a later Secret Service report. Allie's father was yet another talented engraver gone wrong. Allie and her sister, Martha, had grown up helping their dad print and pass coney in Indianapolis. Pete McCartney married Martha, and Ben fell for Allie.

Ben and Allie started working together—he made the bills, she carried them to distributors in her straw shopping basket. Secret Service agents tracked the fake money to Mattoon and busted Boyd in his workshop. At the same time, another team of agents burst into a nearby hotel and grabbed Allie Ackman. When detectives searched Allie's basket, they found $30,000 in phony fifties, twenties, and tens.

It was a tight spot, but Ben managed to get both himself

and his girl off the hook by agreeing to hand over a set of plates for printing $50 bills. The beautifully cut plates had taken about a year of painstaking labor to make.

Free again, Ben and Allie were married in Michigan. From 1865 to 1875 the Boyds kept out of sight. Boyd wasn't a show-off like his brother-in-law, Pete; he preferred to lay low and work. And he was so good, so valuable to his business partners, they spared no expense to protect and hide him.

But the Secret Service knew Boyd was still out there somewhere, and they knew he was still working, because his nearly perfect counterfeit money kept showing up all over the Midwest. Boyd's masterpiece was a $5 bill that even some experts couldn't tell was fake. As one official report put it: "He is considered the best letterer on steel in the country, or the world."

After reviewing the case, Secret Service Chief Washburn gave Patrick Tyrrell his new assignment. He was to track down Ben Boyd and get him dead to rights—grab him with incriminating evidence on him. The capture of Boyd,

Washburn said, would snap the backbone of counterfeiting in the United States.

A veteran of the Chicago police department, Tyrrell knew how things worked in the real world. He needed information about Boyd, and he went to the only people who had it—criminals. Tyrrell contacted Ben's old teacher, Nat Kinsey. Kinsey was down on his luck, and ready to sell out an old pal for the right price.

"I am in need of money in the worst way," Kinsey wrote to Tyrrell in one of the many letters they exchanged.

For the next eight months, Tyrrell saw very little of his wife and children in Chicago. Following tips from Kinsey and other paid informers, the operative followed Boyd's winding trail through Wisconsin, Minnesota, Iowa, Missouri, and Illinois. He discovered that Boyd had lived briefly in Decatur, Illinois, as Charles Mitchell, and as B. F. Wilson in Des Moines, Iowa. In September, Tyrrell learned, the so-called B.F. Wilson and his wife had left Iowa for Fulton, Illinois, where they rented a white house near the banks of the Mississippi River.

Tyrrell headed for Fulton. He found the windows of the

Wilsons' house covered by thick green curtains, always drawn. Neighbors said Mrs. Wilson was sometimes seen going to the market, but Mr. Wilson never showed his face. Another man, though, was often seen coming and going.

This other man was Nat Kinsey. He was helping Boyd cut plates—and secretly sending Tyrrell updates from inside his old student's house.

Tyrrell needed to move quickly. But not too quickly. He had Boyd cornered now, and wanted to give his prey time to settle in, to feel safe. He wanted Boyd to start working on a new set of counterfeit plates. He wanted to catch Boyd in the act.

On October 18, Tyrrell rented a hotel room in Lyons, Iowa, across the river from Fulton. He spent a couple days watching Boyd's street, studying the layout of the surrounding blocks. Two days later, Kinsey took the ferry over to Lyons and found Tyrrell in his room. Good news, Kinsey said. Boyd had started work on a new set of $20 plates.

Tyrrell and Kinsey set their plan. The next morning,

U. S. Treasury Department,

SECRET-SERVICE DIVISION.

Des Moines District.

Lyons Iowa October 21st 1875

Elmer Washburn Esqr
Chief of the U.S.S.D.
                    Sir

         I have the honor to
submit my report as Chief Operator of this
District for the 21st day of October 1875;
This morning in company with James L Brooks
and John McDonald of Chicago, we start
across the River to Fulton, each is assigned
a certain duty, and at 9 oclock all is ready
at the place designated, after a few minutes
delay, his, appears and gives me the signal
agreed upon, promptly each takes the place
assigned, I enter, the door being left open
by his, and in the Dining Room I meet
Mrs Boyd, giving her in charge of Brooks
I proceed up stairs and meet Benjamin
Boyd, at the head of the stairs I inform

---

*A page from Tyrrell's daily
report to Chief Washburn*

Kinsey would be at the house. As Tyrrell approached, Kinsey would signal from the window, letting the operative know whether or not Boyd was at work on his plates. If he was, the raid would proceed. If not, they'd wait. Tyrrell handed Kinsey a twenty, and told him that if all went well they would not speak again.

In his daily report to Chief Washburn, he wrote: "I then arranged to make the pull at 9 o'clock tomorrow morning."

Chapter 2
THE PULL

Early the next morning, Tyrrell tucked his revolver into its holster and left his hotel room. With him were two other armed men in suits, Secret Service agents James Brooks and John McDonald. They walked to the waterfront, got on a ferry, and headed across the Mississippi River.

A few minutes before 9:00, Tyrrell and the other operatives approached Boyd's house on foot. Kinsey leaned out an upstairs window and gave the go-ahead signal.

Tyrrell opened the fence gate in front of the house and walked around toward the back door. Brooks followed close behind, while McDonald hung back to cover the front door.

Suddenly a man raced up in a wagon and screamed, loud enough to be heard inside the house:

"Does B. F. Wilson live here?"

Then the driver took off without waiting for an answer.

Instantly Tyrrell knew—they'd been spotted by Boyd's friends, and that shouted question was a warning to Boyd.

Yelling for the others to stay outside and watch the exits, Tyrrell sprinted to the back door. Just as he was reaching for the doorknob, a man stumbled out, almost crashing into Tyrrell on his way down the steps. It was Kinsey, on his way out.

Tyrrell charged through the empty kitchen and into the dining room, running full-speed into Allie Boyd. Allie grabbed Tyrrell's coat collar, trying to keep him in the room.

"Brooks!" shouted Tyrrell, yanking the woman's strong hands off his collar.

James Brooks bolted in and Tyrrell shoved Allie into his arms. Then Tyrrell spun and ran to the stairs, and was just starting up when he stopped short. Standing at the top of the steps with a startled look on his face was Benjamin Boyd.

Tyrrell pulled out his pistol and said, "Boyd, you are my prisoner."

"Who are you?" growled Boyd.

"United States Detective Tyrrell."

"I have heard of you, Tyrrell," Boyd said, glaring down at the agent.

Tyrrell walked up the steps, holstering his revolver. He slapped handcuffs on Boyd's wrists, then shouted out the window for McDonald, still in the yard, to come inside. While McDonald and Brooks guarded the prisoners, Tyrrell began the search for incriminating evidence.

It was everywhere.

The spare bedroom upstairs was clearly being used as a workroom—there was a large table, with engraving tools scattered around, as if the worker had just been interrupted. More tools were piled in crates on the floor. Tyrrell lifted a black metal plate from the worktable. Cut into the metal was the partially finished design of the front of a U.S. $20 bill. On the desk, right beside where the plate had been, was a real $20 bill.

Tyrrell hurried into town to telegraph the good news to Chief Washburn. When he returned to the house to search the downstairs, McDonald reported an interesting development. While Tyrrell was gone, Allie Boyd had offered McDonald $1,000 in cash to let her take something out of the house.

Tyrrell turned to Allie. What was it she didn't want him to find?

She hesitated, sighed, and pointed to a box in the corner. Tyrrell searched it and found nothing interesting. Then he noticed the box had a fat wooden handle. He cracked it open. Inside, in a tightly rolled bundle, was $7,824 in real U.S. currency.

The search went on for six more hours. "I found a small box," Tyrrell reported. "On breaking it up I found a front and back for a one hundred dollar treasury note." Wrapped in a coat under the Boyds' bed he found partly finished and blank metal plates. In a crate, under a pile of rags, was a plate expertly engraved with the back of a $20 bill—the reverse side of the plate found on Ben's desk.

That afternoon Tyrrell and the other agents packed up the evidence and headed to the train station with their prisoners. They all sat together on the train back to Chicago.

Ben Boyd kept glancing at the crate of counterfeit plates

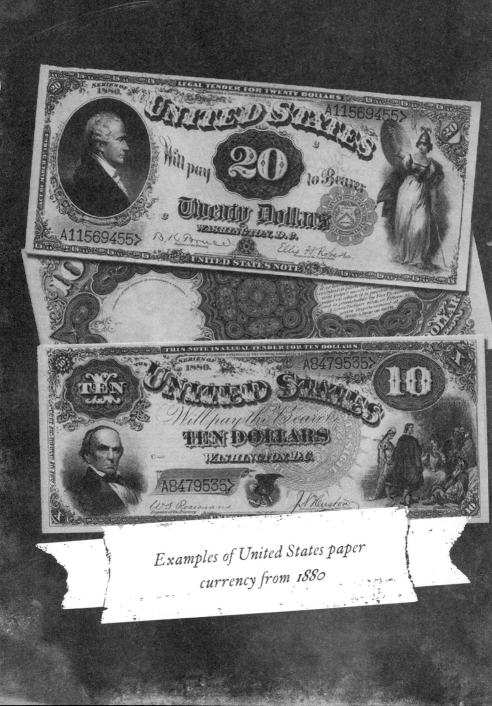

Examples of United States paper currency from 1880

by Tyrrell's feet. There was enough evidence in there to put him away for a long stretch. He turned to the operative.

"Tyrrell," Boyd began, "you are not long in the Secret Service, are you?"

"No, not long," Tyrrell answered. "Why? Anything the matter?"

"Oh, I thought if you were an old member of the Service, you would take the property now in your possession and let me skip out the back door."

Tyrrell shook his head. "But that is not my way of doing business."

Boyd figured as much. Like other counterfeiters, he'd bribed his way out of jams before. But these new Secret Service agents were annoyingly honest.

As if to prove the point, Tyrrell asked Boyd what he wanted done with the money that had been hidden in the hollow box handle. Boyd asked that it be put in the bank, for use by his defense lawyer. To Boyd's amazement, Tyrrell deposited every penny.

Boyd was convinced he wasn't going to be able to buy his freedom.

Plan B was to escape. While awaiting trial in Cook County jail, Boyd and another counterfeiter in the cell tried to make a key to the cell lock. A guard found the half-cut key and confiscated it.

It was beginning to look like Ben Boyd was going to spend a very long time behind bars.

An example of counterfeit currency

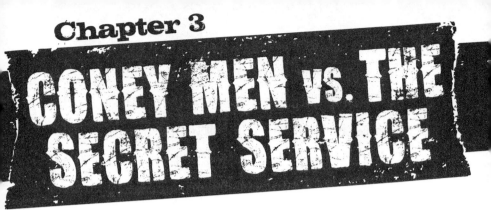

Chapter 3

CONEY MEN vs. THE SECRET SERVICE

It began with seashells.

The earliest form of American-made money was wampum—beads made from white and purple seashells, and strung into decorative belts by Native Americans of the Northeast. Back in the early 1600s, before colonies had their own coins or paper bills, settlers and Indians used wampum belts as a form of currency. The belts could be exchanged for different amounts of goods, depending on size and design. Purple beads, for instance, were worth a bit more than white, because the shells needed to make them were harder to find. Pretty soon, America's first counterfeiters were dying white shells and passing them off as purple.

The colony of Massachusetts was the first to set up a mint, and began issuing silver coins in 1652. Counterfeiters immediately began making pewter copies.

The same happened with early paper currency, thanks to resourceful folks like Mary Butterworth of Rehoboth, Massachusetts. Butterworth, a mother of seven, used the family kitchen as her workroom. First she'd get her iron good and hot in the fire. Then she'd put a genuine paper bill on the table and cover it with a damp cloth. As she ran the iron over the cloth, some of the ink from the money was transferred to the cloth. Quickly and carefully, she laid the cloth on a blank piece of paper and pressed down hard with her iron. This transferred the ink from the cloth to the paper, leaving a perfect outline of the original currency's design. Butterworth always threw her used cloths into the fire after using them. The final step was to use a fine quill pen to darken the design on the fake bill, and fill in the lettering.

Beginning in about 1715, Butterworth spent seven years producing a fortune in counterfeit Rhode Island, Massachusetts, and Connecticut currency. Her brothers and other relatives acted as distributors, selling the bills for half their face value—unusually high for coney, which means that her fakes were of very high quality. The bills were finally noticed and traced to her house, but the court-ordered search turned up no evidence. It was all in ashes in her kitchen fireplace.

In the decades after the American Revolution, the U.S. government produced gold and silver coins, but no national paper currency. Counterfeiters didn't mind—coins were easier to fake. Simply take a real coin and make a mold of the design. Then melt a cheap metal, pour it into the mold, let it harden, and cover the fake coin with a thin plate of real gold or silver. Those who really cared about doing quality work took the extra time to give their coins a handled, tarnished look by rubbing them with sawdust and burning them with fire.

The process wasn't technically challenging, but each coin took time, and each required genuine gold or silver. Counterfeiting coins was a small-time criminal enterprise. As a result, fake coins weren't a huge problem—in 1860, the government figured that less than 2 percent of the coins in circulation were phony.

Counterfeiting went big-time during the Civil War,

which started in 1861. As war ripped the country apart, the U.S. government suddenly needed piles of cash to pay millions of soldiers and buy supplies for the massive Union Army. Congress responded with the Legal Tender Act, and President Abraham Lincoln signed it into law. The new law gave the U.S. Treasury the power to print paper currency. Government printing presses started pumping out hundreds of millions of dollars.

And counterfeiters started copying it.

Making fake paper money was a lot trickier than making coins. For a successful operation, you needed a whole network of distributors and shovers to spread the coney in various cities. You needed lots of cash to put together the team, and to pay for the most vital member—a talented, experienced engraver. But none of this discouraged coney men, since the potential payoff was so great. By 1864 an astounding 50 percent of the paper money in circulation was fake.

This was becoming a gigantic problem for honest business owners. Say you own a store, and a guy comes in and buys five dollars' worth of stuff. He pays with a twenty, and you give him fifteen dollars in change. But then, when you go to put the twenty in the bank, they tell you it's coney—worthless. So you've lost the five bucks' worth of goods and the fifteen you gave in change.

Americans were beginning to lose faith in the green slips of paper. And if citizens stopped trusting the currency, there'd be no way for the government to pay for the war. The entire economy would collapse. A very frightened Treasury Department responded in 1865 by creating the Secret Service, and charging the agency with leading the fight against counterfeiters. Today we think of Secret Service agents as the guys in dark suits protecting the president, but that happened later. Abraham Lincoln was assassinated in 1865, then President James Garfield in 1881, and then President William McKinley in 1901. Only *then* did it occur to Congress that someone should be guarding the president, and they gave the job to the Secret Service.

Back in the 1870s, the one and only task of the Secret Service was to stop the counterfeiters.

On January 19, 1876, Ben and Allie Boyd went on trial in

Secret Service agents in 1865

a Chicago courtroom packed with spectators. As Tyrrell and others testified against the defendants, Allie held a handkerchief to her eyes, weeping pathetically. For some reason, the judge bought her act.

"After hearing the evidence in the case," Tyrrell grumbled, "the judge ordered the jury to find Almiranda Boyd not guilty, it being conceded that she was the wife of Benjamin Boyd and that as such she had only done what was her duty to her husband by covering up his guilt as much as possible."

Allie was acquitted, but the jury took just twenty minutes to find Ben Boyd guilty. The judge sentenced him to ten years in Joliet State Prison.

The conviction was a huge win for the Secret Service. As a reward for busting Boyd, Chief Washburn promoted Tyrrell to chief operative of the Chicago District of the Secret Service, covering the states of Illinois, Missouri, and Wisconsin. A nice honor, but it wasn't going to make his life any easier.

Tyrrell hung a map of his vast territory on the wall of his Chicago office. With just a few agents working under him, he was now responsible for a chunk of land the size of a small country. There were a lot of coney men still out there, Tyrrell knew, and they were sure to strike back.

But in a million years, he never could have guessed how they were going to do it.

Chapter 4
BIG JIM

Three hundred miles to the southwest, in St. Louis, Missouri, a livery stable owner named James Kennally followed the news from Chicago with increasing alarm. He had good reason to be worried. The arrest and conviction of Ben Boyd threatened to bring his entire empire crashing down.

Kennally was thirty-seven years old in 1876. Thanks to descriptions in his prison records, we know he was just under six feet tall, with a fair complexion and light gray eyes. He'd done time in prison for horse theft, and two long stints in the Illinois State Penitentiary for passing counterfeit cash. All that time behind bars taught Kennally some valuable lessons—valuable, that is, to a man determined to continue a life of crime.

Kennally settled in St. Louis and opened a livery stable with a bit of help from an old friend, none other than Ben

Illinois State Penitentiary

Boyd's brother-in-law, Pete McCartney. But Kennally and his investor had no intention of eking out a living by renting horses. The stable was really just a front, making it appear to the world that these men were legitimate businessmen. In fact, behind the scenes, Kennally set up and managed one of the biggest counterfeiting networks in the Midwest. That's when people started calling him "Big Jim."

Big Jim had one strict rule: He never touched the stuff himself. Rather than handling piles of potentially incriminating coney, he accepted orders from counterfeiting gangs around the region. Kennally would then contact an engraver and printer, paying them to produce the needed product. When the coney was ready, he'd have the printer hide the stash in some predetermined spot—in a hollow log out in the country, or in a hole under a roadside rock. The client would be told to pick up his order, and to leave his payment.

Of course, Kennally only accepted payment in real U.S. currency.

It was all wildly profitable, but the entire operation was based on one simple fact: Kennally produced the best, most realistic-looking coney available. And he was able to do this for one simple reason: He hired the best engraver, Ben Boyd.

Boyd's arrest knocked Kennally's system out of joint, and the supply of quality coney circulating in Midwestern cities began to fall. Bank tellers were among the first to notice. Specially trained to detect counterfeit bills, they were used to spotting about one bogus bill an hour. Now, in the early months of 1876, they might see one a month. New tellers were actually upset by the change. As one banker explained,

"Younger men in the bank complained that there was not enough counterfeit money in circulation for them to learn how to detect it."

For young tellers this was an inconvenience; for Big Jim it was a catastrophe. He continued taking orders and producing coney, but everything was harder without Ben Boyd. Other engravers just weren't as talented or meticulous. Fake bills printed from their plates were easier to detect, so they had a shorter life expectancy. For example, say Kennally sold his clients a new batch of $10 bills. Once the police spotted one of these fake tens, they'd distribute descriptions of the bogus bill to business owners and newspapers. That made all the bills in the entire batch just about worthless. Besides, trying to pass inferior coney was a lot riskier than passing top-notch stuff—shovers were much more likely to get caught in the act.

Naturally, Kennally's clients were not about to pay top dollar for lower-quality, riskier merchandise. They demanded steep discounts, and Big Jim had no choice but to agree. His business was falling apart.

"The men who made their living mainly by means of

Boyd's work have been down in the mouth ever since his arrest," declared the *Chicago Tribune*. "They have used every means in their power to get him out." The *Tribune* reporter heard that Boyd's friends had tried to bribe court officials and prison guards, with no luck. "Money could not obtain a pardon," the paper explained. Kennally was getting desperate.

In early March, he got on a train and rode to Lincoln, Illinois, a town named for the country's sixteenth president. There he met with members of the Logan County Gang, regular customers of his. In flush times the gang liked to brag that, thanks to them, there was more bogus than real money floating around Logan County. But business was slow now. The men were eager for any kind of work.

And it just so happened that Big Jim had a job for them. He wanted them to steal the body of Abraham Lincoln.

Incredibly, Big Jim wasn't the first person to think of stealing a dead president.

On a foggy night back in 1830, a young gardener snuck onto the grounds of Mount Vernon, George Washington's

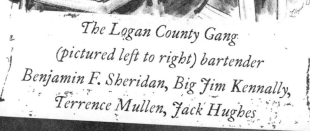

The Logan County Gang
(pictured left to right) bartender
Benjamin F. Sheridan, Big Jim Kennally,
Terrence Mullen, Jack Hughes

Virginia estate (Washington had died in 1799, but the property still belonged to his family). Until a few days before, the gardener had worked at Mount Vernon, but he'd been fired for some unknown reason. Apparently he was pretty upset about the dismissal.

The man felt his way between trees along the soggy ground sloping down from the family house to the banks of the Potomac River. Ahead he saw a small stone building. Exactly what he'd come for: George Washington's burial vault.

The gardener pushed through the unlocked door and stood inside. Fog and faint moonlight slanted in through the crumbling stone walls. Looking around, the man saw twenty coffins. A few lay across wooden beams; others were just stacked on top of each other. The purpose of the vault was to keep the bodies of Washington and his extended family above the often-flooding waters of the Potomac. But the vault's intense heat and humidity were causing the wooden coffins to rot and collapse. Several bones had already fallen to the muddy floor. Only the bodies of George and Martha Washington were well protected inside coffins of lead, lying

The entrance to George Washington's tomb at Mount Vernon

side by side on a wooden table in the corner.

The gardener either didn't know this, or was in too big a hurry, or simply couldn't see much in the dark space. He grabbed what he believed to be George Washington's skull, tucked it under his arm, and ran for home.

The missing body part was discovered the next day and everyone suspected the disgruntled gardener. He was immediately caught, and must have been disappointed to learn he'd actually stolen the skull of one of Washington's in-laws. It was returned, unharmed, to its resting place.

Then, just to make sure, Washington's nephew opened George's coffin and took a look inside. He was still in there. Relieved, the family began building a solid, secure brick tomb for George and Martha. You can still visit this one today.

Thirty-seven years later, in 1867, a lawyer in Springfield, Illinois, had a similar idea. His plan, according to two young men he tried to recruit for the job, was to break into the tomb of Abraham Lincoln and steal his coffin. Then he would stash the body somewhere in the South and wait for ransom offers, returning the body to the highest bidder.

But no one agreed to help the lawyer. He abandoned the scheme, and died a few years later. Only rumors of his plot remained.

Did Big Jim Kennally know these stories? Was he inspired by them? There's no way to know. Certainly, he knew about the crime of body snatching, which was a serious problem in the 1860s and '70s. Medical colleges were always in need of bodies for use in human anatomy classes. Schools were willing to pay cash for bodies, no questions asked—and body snatchers filled the demand by digging up and delivering fresh corpses.

Big Jim's plan was a bit more ambitious. And the payment he expected was a bit higher than the typical fifteen dollars paid by colleges.

Following Kennally's detailed instructions, Logan County Gang leader Thomas Sharp picked four other gang members. The five-man team traveled by wagon thirty miles north to Springfield, Illinois, Abraham Lincoln's former home—and the location of his tomb.

The men rented a two-story building downtown. They

opened a saloon on the first floor, and turned the second floor into a dance hall. This gave the team a perfect front for their operation. Gang member Robert Splain worked as a bartender, and the other members drifted in one at a time, just like regular customers. They could meet and talk at the bar without attracting any attention. For particularly secret sessions, they could duck into the back room.

Kennally's orders were to break into Lincoln's tomb, snatch his body, and bury it in a ditch along the Sangamon River a few miles north of town. The disappearance of Lincoln's remains would be front-page news all over the country, of course. The government would offer a huge reward for the return of the body. This is where Big Jim planned to make a personal appearance in the story. Only after the body was planted, Kennally was to travel from St. Louis to Springfield. While doing a little fishing in the Sangamon River, he'd just happen to stumble on Lincoln's shallow grave.

Sure, the police would find Kennally's chance discovery extremely suspicious. But Kennally would have a rock-solid alibi—he was in St. Louis on the night of the theft, with eyewitnesses to prove it. His innocence established, he'd offer to return the body. For the right price, naturally.

To get back Lincoln's body, the government was going to have to let Ben Boyd out of jail.

Big Jim's final touch was the date of the theft: the night of July 3. It was the night before Independence Day, and not just any Independence Day. July 4, 1876, would be the country's one hundredth birthday—exactly one century from the day Congress approved the Declaration of Independence. By the night of July 3, the celebration in town would be well underway; no one would notice a few strangers lurking around Lincoln's tomb. And on July 4, people in Springfield would be so busy with parades and fireworks that they wouldn't notice Lincoln was missing—giving Kennally's crew plenty of time to slip safely out of town.

Thomas Sharp and the gang prepared carefully for the big night. One by one, on different days, each man took the two-mile streetcar ride from downtown Springfield to Oak Ridge Cemetery. Each paid the twenty-five-cent admission fee and walked up a muddy path toward the Lincoln Monument.

Chapter 5

FIRST TRY

Abraham Lincoln had traveled a long and strange road to this resting place.

Eleven years before, in April 1865, things had finally been looking up for Lincoln. After the bloodiest four years in American history, the Civil War was over. Congress had passed the Thirteenth Amendment to the Constitution, declaring a permanent end to slavery.

On the afternoon of April 14, Abraham and his wife, Mary, went for a carriage ride in Washington, DC, and he spent the whole

Mary Todd Lincoln

time happily greeting people on the street.

"Dear husband," Mary said, "you almost startle me by your great cheerfulness."

"And well may I feel so," said Abe. "I never felt so happy in my life."

That night they went to see a comedy at Ford's Theatre. A few minutes after 10:00, John Wilkes Booth snuck into Lincoln's box and shot the president in the head. Lincoln never regained consciousness, and he died the next morning. His body was taken back to the White House and carried up to a second-floor guest room.

Dr. Edward Curtis walked into the room later that morning. Small groups of generals and political leaders stood around, talking in whispers. On a table, covered in white sheets, lay Lincoln's body. With a room full of people looking on, Curtis and another surgeon began the autopsy. They sawed off the top of the skull and inspected the brain. The hole made by Booth's bullet was clearly visible, but the bullet itself was not.

"We proceeded to remove the entire brain," Curtis later reported. "Suddenly the bullet dropped out through my

Lincoln's assassination at Ford's Theatre by John Wilkes Booth

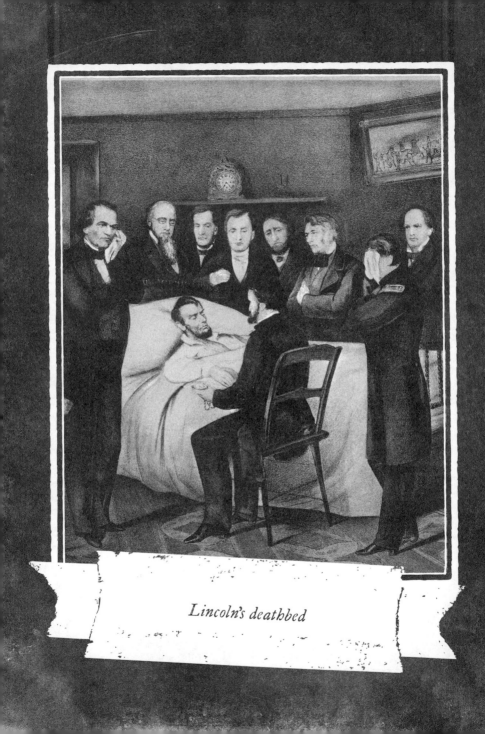

Lincoln's deathbed

fingers and fell, breaking the solemn silence of the room with its clatter, into an empty basin that was standing beneath."

When the autopsy was finished, an undertaker named Charles Brown and his best embalmer, Henry Cattell, were shown into the room. Their job was to make the body look as good as possible—for as long as possible. They replaced the top of Lincoln's head. Brown closed Lincoln's eyes and lifted the corners of his mouth so it almost looked like he was smiling.

Cattell drained the blood from Lincoln's body and pumped in embalming fluid, a mix of chemicals that preserved the body and hardened it, making the face appear more like marble than skin. The body was then dressed in one of Lincoln's best black suits, and placed in a coffin.

Secretary of War Edwin Stanton came in to look everything over, and saw that the skin on the president's face was badly bruised from the impact of the bullet that had killed him.

Someone in the room asked if the undertaker should try and hide the bruising.

Lincoln lying in state at the Capitol building in Washington, DC

"No," Stanton said. "This is part of the history of the event."

After lying in an open coffin (or "lying in state") in the Capitol building for two days, Lincoln's body was placed on a train for the long ride home to Illinois. The train stopped in cities along the way for massive memorial ceremonies. It's estimated that more than one and a half million Americans filed past to see Lincoln's body. Between cities, the funeral

Lincoln's funeral train

train rolled along at just five miles an hour, and crowds of people lined the tracks, night and day, all the way west.

Meanwhile, in Springfield, a battle was brewing over the body. Mary Todd Lincoln insisted her husband be laid to rest in a quiet cemetery away from the center of town—it's what he had told her he wanted. But Lincoln's friends argued he should be buried right in the city, with a grand tomb and memorial for all to see. They even bought a property and began drawing up plans. Mary got so upset that she threatened to take the body out of Springfield and bury it in Chicago instead. That won her the argument.

When the funeral train pulled into Springfield on the morning of May 3, Lincoln's body was carried from the railroad station to the State House. Charles Brown had traveled all the way with the body, making sure it was ready for each public viewing. Now, as thousands gathered to see their fallen hero, Brown and a local undertaker named Thomas Lynch opened the coffin to make sure everything was all right. They were horrified. The bruising on Lincoln's face had grown much worse. They couldn't let him be seen this way.

Funeral procession in Chicago for Lincoln

Lynch hurried out, pushing through crowds in the hallway. "I called at a neighborhood drugstore," he explained, "and procured a rouge chalk and amber, with such brushes as I needed, and returned to the room."

Expertly applying the color of living flesh to Lincoln's face, Lynch hid the bruises. "In half an hour I had finished my task and the doors were thrown open to the public." The body was on view in the State House all day and night. The next morning, Abraham Lincoln's coffin was closed, and, according to Mary's wishes, the body was taken out to Oak Ridge Cemetery.

Lincoln's Springfield friends still wanted Lincoln to have a majestic tomb. So they formed a group called the Lincoln Monument Association, raised money, and built a monument at Oak Ridge. The Lincoln Monument was completed in 1874, and the president's coffin was moved inside. Lincoln's remains could finally rest in peace—or so everyone believed.

When Thomas Sharp and his gang came to check out the Lincoln Monument, the first thing they saw was a tall

The Lincoln Monument being built

obelisk—a needle-shaped tower of gray granite. The tower rose from the center of a square building made of the same light stone. The whole thing sat on the top of a low, grassy hill, surrounded by trees.

In charge of the place was a bearded, fifty-seven-year-old man named John Carroll Power. As official custodian of the Lincoln Monument, Power earned fifty dollars a month to take care of the monument and lead tours of the tomb. He personally greeted every visitor—including each of the Logan County Gang members. They seemed to him like typical tourists. "All visited the monument, and mingled with other visitors," he would later write.

John Carroll Power

Power showed guests into the structure, explaining that the main entrance opened into an oval chamber called Memorial Hall. The custodian had turned this into a homemade Lincoln museum, setting up glass cases and filling them with various Lincoln-related items from his personal collection. There were letters from Lincoln, photos, a copy of the Emancipation Proclamation, even surveying tools Lincoln had used as a young man. But the prize of the collection was a bloody strip of fabric. Moments after Lincoln was shot in Ford's Theatre, an actress named Laura Keene ran from the stage to Lincoln's box and cradled the head of the dying president. Years later, Power paid twenty-five dollars for a piece of Keene's bloodstained dress—and put it on display in Memorial Hall.

An interesting little show, but the Logan County boys saw no sign of a coffin. Several of them asked Power where Lincoln's body was.

It was a question Power got all the time, and not one that aroused suspicion. He explained that on the other side of the building, about 150 feet from Memorial Hall, was a second, smaller room—the tomb chamber, or "catacomb," as Power called it.

Power led his guests outside and around the monument to the catacomb. Two locked doors guarded the small room. The first was wood, with a glass window. It was a joke, the gang saw—you could simply kick it in, or break the glass. The second, inner door was a gate of thick steel bars, secured with a padlock. That would be more of an obstacle, but hardly discouraging.

Through the doors, guests could dimly see to the far wall of the catacomb, where there were five closet-sized crypts. The bodies of Lincoln's dead sons rested in three of the crypts; the empty ones were for Lincoln's one living son,

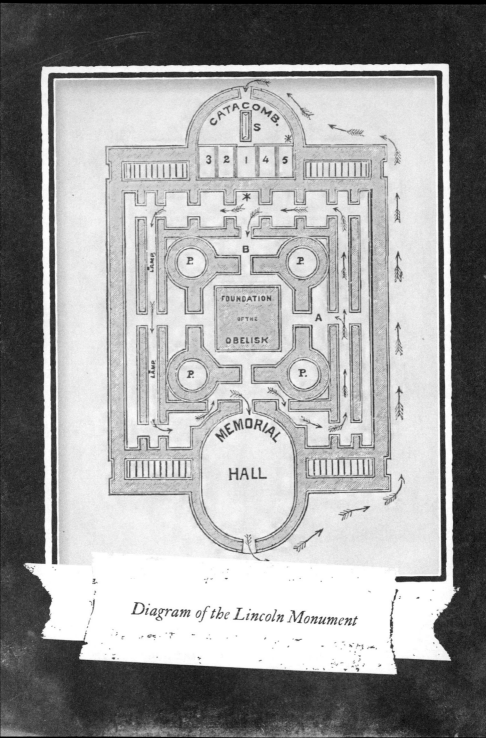

Diagram of the Lincoln Monument

Robert, and his wife, Mary. In the middle of the floor sat a large marble sarcophagus, or casket. Inside the sarcophagus was a coffin made of red cedar. Inside of that was an airtight coffin of thick lead. Inside of that was Lincoln's body.

Each gang member had a look, and heard some version of Power's presentation. To be sure he'd understood, one of them asked Power if the body was really right there, above ground.

Yes, said Power. The room had a tile floor, and the marble sarcophagus rested on the tiles.

Another gang member asked if he could take a look inside, just out of curiosity.

Sorry, Power apologized, no visitors allowed in the catacomb.

How about a night guard? Surely someone stayed in there at night to keep watch?

No, said Power, there was no night watchman, either at the tomb or in the surrounding cemetery.

The gang members met back at their saloon in Springfield. It all looked good, they agreed. Even easier than expected.

There would be no digging required, which simplified things. They just needed to break through a couple of locks, crack open the stone sarcophagus, and yank out the cedar coffin—it'd be heavy with the lead box inside, but doable with five men. They'd load it into a wagon, drive to the river, and bury it in the spot chosen by Kennally: a gravel bar under a bridge a few miles out of town. Then, while the nation celebrated Independence Day, they'd scatter and disappear.

By early June the gang had all the details worked out, all the tools ready. The only thing left to do was wait for the big night.

That turned out to be the hardest part.

"Until that time, all had gone along smoothly," John Carroll Power later wrote. "Each and all had kept their secrets, and not a shadow of suspicion had been aroused."

But now, with three weeks to kill, the men started hanging around in bars, drinking heavily and trying to impress the women of Springfield. One night Thomas Sharp got drunk and started crowing about a big deal he had in the works. While everyone else was shooting off fireworks,

Map of the Lincoln Monument grounds

he bragged, "I'm gonna be out at Oak Ridge stealing old Lincoln's bones!"

A woman named Belle Bruce turned to Sharp in shock. Was he really serious?

Sharp assured her he was.

Later that night Bruce repeated Sharp's strange tale to Abner Wilkinson, Springfield's chief of police. Wilkinson ran into John Carroll Power on the street the next morning.

"He told me confidentially," recalled Power, "that in the discharge of his official duties, he had discovered a plot to steal the remains of President Lincoln."

Meanwhile, Belle Bruce must have told a few other folks Sharp's wild story, because within a day it was all over town. The rumors quickly got back to Sharp himself. Sober now, Sharp must have cursed his stupidity. It was safe to assume the police already knew about his plans; he'd blown the job.

The Logan County Gang lugged everything movable out of the saloon, loaded it onto a wagon, and raced out of town. All they left behind was an unpaid rent bill.

"Whisky alone is entitled to the credit of having thwarted this well-laid scheme to steal the remains of President Lincoln," recalled John Carroll Power. But the maddening thing was that the custodian couldn't get anyone to pay attention to the close call. The whole city seemed focused on preparing for the country's one hundredth birthday.

And then, just two days after Independence Day, shocking news arrived by telegram from the West. "HORRIBLE!" screamed the headline of the *Chicago Tribune* on July 6, 1876. "General Custer Attacks an Indian Camp with Five Companies, and All Perish."

Ten days before, on the banks of the Little Bighorn River in Montana, U.S. soldiers led by George Armstrong Custer had clashed with Lakota and Cheyenne warriors. The Indian fighters quickly surrounded Custer and more than two hundred of his men, and wiped out the entire American force. In the ongoing wars along the western frontier, this was by far the worst defeat ever suffered by the U.S. Army.

As Americans began to recover from the shock of Little Bighorn, the country's interest turned to the next big news story—the presidential election, set for November. The Republicans nominated Ohio governor Rutherford B.

Hayes; the Democrats picked Samuel J. Tilden, governor of New York. This was shaping up to be the most hotly contested election since the Civil War, and by late summer the nasty campaigning was well underway.

With so much going on, no one was too concerned with the bizarre rumors floating around Springfield, Illinois. No one but John Carroll Power, that is. He went directly to his bosses, the leaders of the Lincoln Monument Association, and told them what he knew about the plot to steal Lincoln. "It seemed to them so incredible," he recalled, "that no attention was given to it."

Basically, Lincoln's old friends didn't believe the story.

Rutherford B. Hayes   *Samuel Tilden*

They told Power to forget the whole thing.

And the fact is, Power's job was a big enough headache without the worry of body snatchers. The Lincoln monument had been built so badly that pieces were already falling off, and on rainy days, drops trickled through the stone roof onto visitors' heads. That's assuming they could make it up the muddy paths to the tomb.

So Power got back to work. And everything drifted back to normal in Springfield.

Big Jim Kennally watched it all from the safe distance of St. Louis. Sure, he was stewing with fury at the Logan County Gang for their boneheaded blunder. The idiots had blown a golden opportunity—but the good news was, no one seemed to have noticed. Big Jim was convinced his idea could still work.

Kennally sold his St. Louis stable, packed up his bags, and bought a train ticket for Chicago. He was part-owner of a saloon there. That's where he could find the men he wanted to see.

Kennally didn't believe he needed a better plan. He just needed a better team.

A young man named Jack Hughes strolled the bustling streets of Chicago, in no particular hurry. Hughes wore a well-tailored suit, and the skin of his face was nearly covered with a bristly mustache and thick black beard. Hughes stepped into a store, picked up a few small items, and brought them to the counter. He handed over a counterfeit bill, accepted change in genuine currency, thanked the clerk, and walked out with a nice little profit.

This was the "boodle game"—a favorite technique of expert shovers like Jack Hughes.

Jack Hughes

It worked like this. Hughes carried a roll of paper money in his pocket, all genuine except for one counterfeit bill. Half a block behind him followed his boodle carrier, a kid of about seventeen, with a pocket full of coney. When Hughes entered a store, the kid hung around near the entrance, in earshot of the front counter. Hughes bought something, didn't matter what, and paid with his fake bill. If the clerk didn't detect the coney, he'd give change in real money. If the clerk did detect it, Hughes would snatch the bill back, and apologize politely.

"Why, that's funny," he'd say, clearly embarrassed. "I don't know where I got it!"

Then he'd pull out his stack of real money and pay with a legitimate bill.

All the while, the boodle carrier watched and listened for trouble. If the clerk made a scene, threatening to call the cops, the kid would take off. He'd be long gone—carrying the incriminating evidence with him—before the law could arrive. Hughes could show the cops his real money, explaining that he must have gotten the one bogus bill for change somewhere. That happened to honest folks all the time.

But if everything went smoothly, Hughes and the kid would meet for just an instant outside the store. The kid handed over a single counterfeit bill, which Hughes put in his pocket with the real ones. And then they headed for a new store and did the routine all over again, repeating the process until they'd successfully shoved the whole stack of coney.

When Hughes needed a new stash of counterfeit cash, he headed to West Madison Street. He walked along the busy street, past dressmakers, tailors, fortune-tellers, billiard halls, a druggist, and a photographer, and slipped into his favorite saloon, a place called the Hub.

Stepping through the front door, Hughes stood in a large, dark room. A layer of sawdust covered the wood plank floors. A lot of beer was spilled in this place, and customers sometimes spit on the floor—the sawdust absorbed it all and kept people from slipping.

Small groups of men sat at mismatched chairs and tables scattered around the space. A few more leaned over the billiard tables in the back, lining up shots. Hughes walked to the long bar and could see his bearded face in the large mirror hanging on the back wall. On a little shelf by the mirror was a plaster bust of Abraham Lincoln.

Hughes greeted the bartender, a young man with shiny black hair and a bushy mustache and quick, darting eyes that took in everything. This was Terrence Mullen, part-owner of the place. Mullen lived in a couple of rooms in the back. He kept his pet, a snake, in a box on the bar. Not poisonous, he assured patrons.

The Hub was a perfect setup for Mullen. He made a little money selling liquor and cold beer while distracting the law from his real business: distributing counterfeit money. Shovers like Hughes drifted in and out, just like hundreds of other regular customers. Mullen slipped his trusted shovers the coney and took his payment in good, honest cash.

Like most coney men, Mullen had a long criminal record for passing fake money.

Terrence Mullen

He walked around with a pistol tucked in his belt, and was considered dangerous by the Chicago police. "Will shoot without a very extraordinary amount of provocation," warned one official report.

Secret Service operative Patrick Tyrrell was aware of the Hub, and had a pretty good idea of what went on there. But the Hub was just one of more than 2,500 saloons doing business in Chicago, many of which were suspected of shady dealings. The Secret Service could hardly watch them all.

Then Tyrrell got an unexpected break. The Chicago police had tailed a teenage kid well known to the cops as a boodle carrier. They collared the kid with pockets stuffed full of coney. Desperate to lighten his sentence, he offered to talk. He'd tell police anything they wanted to know about the shover he worked for, a guy named Jack Hughes.

Tyrrell rushed to the police station to question the kid. Tyrrell knew Hughes by reputation. He knew Hughes had been arrested in Chicago for passing fake fives a year before. Hughes's friends had bailed him out, and Hughes had jumped bail—never showed up for his court hearing.

He'd been out there somewhere ever since, dodging the law, shoving coney all over town.

The young boodle carrier was scared, which made him very helpful to Tyrrell. He told Tyrrell the place to find Jack Hughes was a saloon on West Madison. It was called the Hub.

An excellent tip, but not one Tyrrell could act on himself. If he strolled into the Hub, every crook in the joint would instantly identify him as a cop—he just had that look. Tyrrell needed someone who could gather information inside the Hub and bring it to him. He needed a roper.

Ropers were not quite the same thing as undercover agents. They didn't officially work for the police or Secret Service. In fact, they were usually criminals. The best ropers had been arrested and done time in prison. They knew how criminals talked, and could swap true stories of past offenses.

"As long as they can maintain it," Tyrrell said of ropers, "and are not caught squealing, they can earn an honest living by giving information."

Some people criticized the Secret Service for putting

low-life crooks on the government payroll. But these critics were living in a dreamworld, Tyrrell thought. His job was to catch criminals, and to do that you had to get your hands dirty.

"When men go fishing, the most important thing is to learn what kind of bait the fish they wish to catch will swallow," Tyrrell explained.

He began poking around the Chicago underworld for just the right roper.

Meanwhile, a stranger calling himself "Cornelius" arrived in town and showed up at the Hub. Though the customers didn't know it, this was Mullen's partner in the saloon, and his supplier of coney. The man's real name was James Kennally.

Big Jim did not particularly want to be seen in the Hub. He made a few brief visits, speaking quickly to Mullen, then leaving.

Then, one day in August, Big Jim entered and walked through the saloon to one of the back rooms. Mullen stepped out from behind the bar and joined Kennally. Jack Hughes walked in moments later. Then came Herbert Nelson, a successful freight company owner, and one of Kennally's most trusted coney distributors.

None of the participants kept a record of this closed-door meeting, but we can piece one together based on later events. The men were all in the same boat—the loss of Ben Boyd's talented hands was costing them cash. Without Boyd, the life of a coney man was riskier, and less profitable. Something had to be done.

Kennally told the group about the Logan County Gang's badly botched try for Lincoln's corpse. Rumors of the plot had swirled for a while, but now, a month later, they had died down. No new security had been added at the Lincoln Monument—no extra guards, no new locks, nothing. The body was as vulnerable as ever. Kennally told his handpicked team that they were going to go and get it.

The men were hesitant. They were coney men, not body snatchers.

It would be an easy job, Kennally assured them. Big Jim didn't discuss the fine points of his plan, but he did add one more detail of interest. If they did the job right, in addition to winning Boyd's freedom, the gang would divvy up $200,000 in cash.

That did it—Mullen, Hughes, and Nelson were in.

But over the next few days, Nelson started to get cold feet. He owned a fleet of wagons and made decent money hauling freight around Chicago. It was a good thing, and he didn't want to risk it. Nelson told the others he'd gladly help out in small ways, but wanted no part of the actual heist.

Mullen and Hughes started looking for a new third man.

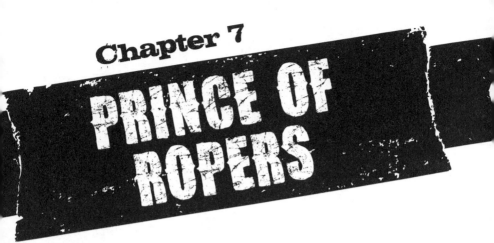

Chapter 7
PRINCE OF ROPERS

Meanwhile, Patrick Tyrrell was still looking for his roper.

Walking along LaSalle Street in downtown Chicago, Tyrrell discussed the problem with his friend Charles Deane. In his work as a lawyer, Deane had occasional dealings with shady characters. He had a possible roper to recommend.

The man's name was Lewis Swegles, though he also went by John Morris and a few other phony names. Swegles was in his late twenties, of average height and build. He was talkative, funny, a natural-born entertainer. He'd grown up in Wisconsin and run off at thirteen to become a sailor. Later, back in the Midwest, he started stealing horses. Like all good ropers, he was known to other criminals and had done time in prison. In the Wisconsin State Penitentiary he'd met plenty of coney men, and had a basic idea of how their world operated. Now Swegles was here in Chicago, married, trying to go straight.

"He's anxious to be employed," Deane assured Tyrrell, "and has knowledge of certain counterfeiters and their operations that might make him valuable."

Tyrrell said he was intrigued. Deane took him to meet the man newspapers would soon proclaim "the Prince of Ropers."

Tyrrell and Swegles talked on the street later that morning.

"Swegles and myself walked around a few blocks," the operative wrote that night in his report to Chief Washburn. "He said that he knew all about the case of Jack Hughes."

That got Tyrrell's attention.

He moved slowly, though, wanting Swegles to understand what he was getting into. As a roper, he'd be expected to worm his way in with Hughes and his pals. Once he had their trust, he could earn money by selling Tyrrell bits of information about their plans. It was a dangerous way to make money, possibly deadly—criminal gangs are not gentle with men caught squealing to the cops.

Swegles understood, and wanted the work.

Tyrrell told him to check out a saloon called the Hub, where Hughes was reputed to hang out.

Swegles went right to the Hub, walked in, and ordered a drink. Just to be friendly, he bought one for the bartender, Terrence Mullen. Mullen took the drink, but kept his distance from Swegles. He never liked to talk much with strangers.

Swegles didn't force it. He dropped into the Hub often over the next couple of weeks. He was always smiling, always telling funny stories to other customers. He let slip a few hints about some time spent in prison, but offered no details.

On August 28, while Swegles was drinking and cracking jokes at the bar, Jack Hughes walked in. One of Swegles's new friends pointed Hughes out. Swegles may not have seemed too interested, but as soon as he finished his drink he left the bar and hurried to Tyrrell's office with the update.

Tyrrell immediately headed over to the Hub, and found Hughes sitting at a table.

"Is all the money in your pocket good money?" Tyrrell demanded.

"Never have any other kind," said Hughes.

Tyrrell told Hughes to empty his pockets. Hughes pulled out six dollars in paper money, and a bit of change. No coney.

Tyrrell hauled Hughes to the police station to face older charges of passing counterfeit currency. The cops photographed Hughes, wrote down his description, and tossed him in jail. His friends quickly raised $2,000 to pay his bail, and by the second week of September, Hughes was back at the Hub.

Hughes's trial was set for the coming January—but he could worry about that later. For now, he and Mullen had important plans to make.

Tyrrell was impressed with his new roper's performance. He offered Swegles the usual roper rate of five dollars a day to continue reporting on the goings-on at the Hub. In particular, Tyrrell wanted some solid evidence to use against Hughes in court, and information about the higher-ups in Hughes's coney ring.

Swegles went back to the Hub. Again playing it cool, he didn't try to approach Hughes directly. Instead he hung around at the bar, where small crowds gathered to hear hilarious tales of his past misadventures. Swegles always made sure to casually weave in the names of criminals he'd worked with or befriended behind bars.

Swegles noticed that Hughes seemed to enjoy his stories. This gave him an opening. He chatted with the shover, casually mentioning that he'd read about Hughes's arrest in the newspaper. He let Hughes know that he was toying with the idea of getting into the coney business himself.

Hughes responded with some vague advice. He didn't know Swegles well, and had no idea if the man was on the level.

Swegles continued patiently working his role. He stayed away from the Hub for a couple of days, then charged back in flashing a wad of greenbacks. He told Hughes and the other Hub regulars that he and his buddy, Billy Brown, had just cleaned out a tannery up in Wisconsin, and made off with a bundle!

Mullen listened with interest from his spot behind the

bar. He and Hughes were still looking for a third man for Big Jim's Lincoln tomb job. Maybe Swegles would fit the bill.

They started asking around about Swegles. The stories he'd told about past arrests seemed to check out. Then, during one of their rare stops at another saloon, Hughes and Mullen spotted a policeman known for bragging about his vast knowledge of criminals. The coney men treated the detective to a few rounds of beer, then asked him what he knew of a man named Lewis Swegles.

The detective proudly announced, "Why, he is one of the biggest horse thieves in the country!"

Hughes and Mullen liked the sound of that.

Through September and into October, the 1876 presidential campaign continued heating up. Back then, candidates didn't travel the country shaking hands and making speeches— that kind of campaigning wouldn't start until 1896 with William McKinley. Before that, newspapers were the main battleground. Competing papers aggressively promoted competing political parties and politicians. And the partisan attacks were every bit as savage as they are today.

Papers backing the Democratic candidate, Samuel J. Tilden, didn't talk much about Tilden. Instead they hammered away at the corruption and scandals that had stained the current Republican president, Ulysses S. Grant. No Republican could be trusted, the Democrats proclaimed, least of all their candidate for president, Rutherford B. Hayes—who as a Union general during the Civil War had possibly stolen the pay of dead soldiers! There was absolutely no basis for this accusation. But Democrats knew that just throwing the charge out there would do some damage to Hayes.

Republican newspapers blasted back with the strategy known as "waving the bloody shirt." They spoke of the horrors of the Civil War and reminded readers that it had been Democratic leaders who had seceded from the Union and fired on the American flag—and Republicans, under Lincoln, who had held the country together. The papers suggested that Democrats were traitors, and their candidate Tilden was no different. Tilden hadn't served in the war, papers pointed out, and was probably still a rebel sympathizer and supporter of slavery. What's more, claimed one paper, Tilden was "a drunkard, a liar, a cheat, a counterfeiter, a perjurer, and a swindler." No evidence was presented.

Terrence Mullen and Jack Hughes were not exactly what you would call civic-minded citizens. It's likely they never voted in their lives. But they couldn't avoid hearing news of the upcoming election, and the fierce campaign would impact their plans in one important way.

But first, they still needed that third man.

Sometime in the middle of October, the coney men pulled Swegles aside at the Hub. In hushed voices, they asked him if he'd like to make a little money.

Maybe, Swegles said. What was the lay?

Body snatching, they told him. A very rich man had just gone toes up in Kenosha, Wisconsin. They were going to go up there, dig up the corpse, and hold it for ransom, figuring the family would pay handsomely to get it back.

Swegles must have been shocked. He thought these guys were finally going to invite him into their coney ring. This grave robbing thing came out of nowhere—and the roper sensed it was some kind of test. He said he needed a little time to think over the offer, maybe to check out the penalty for body snatching in Wisconsin.

Swegles left the bar and walked to the office of Charles Deane, the lawyer who'd gotten him into the roper business. Deane listened to the story. He told Swegles the plan sounded like a "feeler"—Hughes and Mullen probably wanted to see how Swegles would respond. Wait a day or two, Deane suggested, then go back to the Hub and tell them you're not interested.

Swegles followed Deane's advice. Hughes and Mullen didn't seem too upset.

Swegles and Deane had guessed right. The coney man had no intention of digging up corpses in Kenosha—they only proposed the plot to see if Swegles could keep his mouth shut. Rumors flew quickly through the criminal community of Chicago. If Swegles mentioned the Kenosha plan to anyone, the story would get back to the Hub soon enough.

A week passed. Hughes and Mullen heard nothing about a Wisconsin grave robbing plot. Swegles could keep a secret, they decided.

The timing was right. Big Jim was pressuring them to get moving on the Lincoln job.

A few nights later, Hughes and Mullen led Swegles into one of the back rooms of the Hub. They shut the door behind them, and sat down to talk.

Forget the Wisconsin job, Mullen told Swegles. The lay was still grave robbing, Mullen said, but the new idea was "a much bigger thing than the Kenosha rich man."

Mullen explained the plan that he and Hughes had worked out with Big Jim Kennally. They were going to take a train to Springfield, bust into the Lincoln Monument, and steal the coffin holding Lincoln's corpse. They'd load the box onto a wagon and drive it two hundred and twenty miles northeast to the sand dunes along the shore of Lake Michigan. The beauty of the dunes was that wind would quickly blow sand over their wagon tracks.

After the body was stashed in the Indiana sand, Big Jim Kennally would contact authorities. The terms for the return of Lincoln's body would be simple: Boyd's freedom and $200,000 in cash.

Lincoln's monument had cost about $200,000 to build, Mullen cackled. "What is the use of the monument without the corpse!"

Swegles was too stunned to respond.

The silence in the room must have lasted an uncomfortably long time. His friends might think he was losing his nerve. He had to say something.

"I'm the boss body snatcher of Chicago!" Swegles blurted out.

Mullen and Hughes looked intrigued. They knew they liked Swegles, but didn't know he had experience robbing graves.

Swegles saw that he'd said the right thing. He relaxed a bit, his heartbeat slowing. Now he just had to back up his bold lie with a few body snatching stories. We don't know what tales Swegles told, but somehow he convinced his new partners he was an expert on the subject.

The coney men welcomed him to the team.

Chapter 8
THE TRAP

As soon as the meeting was over, Swegles slipped out of the Hub and raced down dark streets toward Tyrrell's office. Mullen and Hughes had said the job would be done very soon, but didn't name a date. So at that moment, Swegles was the only one standing between the coney men and Lincoln's body.

Was he really worried about protecting Lincoln's remains? Or was he thinking he'd lucked into a roper's dream—a nugget of gold that would vastly increase his value in the eyes of the Secret Service? We can't be sure.

Swegles leaped up the stairs to Tyrrell's office. The agent was out of town on another investigation.

The roper couldn't keep this explosive secret to himself. He found his friend Charles Deane and described the Hub gang's bizarre plot.

Deane's advice: sit tight, say nothing, wait for Tyrrell.

But Deane couldn't keep the secret, either. He told Leonard Swett, a fellow Chicago lawyer who'd been one of Abraham Lincoln's closest friends. Alarmed, Swett telegraphed a warning to members of the Lincoln Monument Association in Springfield. Swett explained that he wasn't sure how serious the threat really was, but added: "Perhaps the slightest intimation of danger ought to induce proper safeguards—if the body is in a position where it could possibly be exposed to such a scheme."

The body was most definitely exposed, the Monument Association members knew. They ordered Power to add a night watchman or two at the monument. "And keep them there until the attempt is made, or danger averted."

Power did as he was told. "After that," he later wrote, "two men, armed each with a revolver, were kept there every night." The custodian patrolled the grounds, too, making sure to arrange signals with the guards, so the men could recognize each other in the dark cemetery.

"I was there at nearly all times of night myself, to see that the watchmen were on duty," Power said. "I had to be very

The receiving vault at the
Lincoln Monument

careful about signals to avoid being shot on my own orders."

On October 26, two nights after Swegles first learned of the plot, Tyrrell was back in his Chicago office. He was sitting at his desk, working late into the night on his daily report to James Brooks, the new chief of the Secret Service. The door opened and Swegles charged in.

"Something's brewing down at the Hub!" he announced.

Tyrrell looked up from his papers.

Not a coney job, the roper said. Something much bigger.

Tyrrell listened to a few details, then cut in. He accused Swegles of being drunk.

Swegles denied it. And he provided convincing details, like the fact that Hughes and Mullen had researched the law on grave robbing in Illinois, and were pleased to find the crime was punishable by only one year in county jail.

Tyrrell was stunned. He needed time to think. He told Swegles to play along with Hughes and Mullen—and to keep in close touch.

After Swegles left, Tyrrell picked up his pen and continued his report.

"Now Chief," he began, "last but not least comes a matter reported to me this evening by Lewis Swegles." Tyrrell laid out the incredible story. "Swegles also says they have some jimmies and one crow bar as tools for the job of breaking into the Monument. They feel confident of success, saying that if they do get caught 'tis only one year in jail and if they succeed Ben will be liberated.

"Deeming the matter of national importance if they commit such a damnable act without detection, I thought best to telegraph the facts as I did this evening to you."

Tyrrell sent his telegraph to Washington. Then he tried to get some sleep. In the morning he'd have to go see Abraham Lincoln's son.

Robert Todd Lincoln

At the age of thirty-three, Robert Lincoln had already lived through several lifetimes' worth of drama.

Robert was a college

student when the Civil War broke out, and he wanted to leave school and enlist in the Union Army. His father, the president, approved. His mother did not. The Lincolns had already watched two young sons die of disease, and Mary could not bear the thought of losing their eldest boy. So Robert stayed at Harvard after he graduated in 1864, and entered law school.

But his absence from the army was becoming a national scandal. Newspapers called Robert a draft dodger and a coward. They accused the president of hiding his son in school, while sending other men's boys out to fight and die. Mary finally relented, allowing Robert to join the army in early 1865.

When the fighting ended in April, he returned to Washington, DC. On the night of April 14, he was spending a quiet evening in his White House bedroom when he heard people shouting that his father had just been shot at Ford's Theatre. Jumping into a carriage, he raced to the scene, and was told the president had been taken to a house across the street. He tried to enter, but soldiers blocked the door.

"It's my father!" Robert shouted. "My father!"

Robert stumbled inside, stepping over pools of blood on the floor. Already weeping, he ran to his dying father.

Later that month, Robert moved to Chicago with his mother and younger brother, Tad. Robert finished law school, got married, and had a child of his own. Then Tad got sick and died at the age of eighteen. Robert watched his mother sink into a grief so deep she could barely function.

Fearing she might take her own life if left alone, Robert decided his mother had to be committed to a mental institution. But Mary didn't want to go. Robert needed a court to declare her legally insane. So Mary was dragged into court, and the whole nightmare played out in the newspapers, which painted Robert as a cold-blooded villain for testifying against his heartbroken mother.

"Oh, Robert," Mary cried, "to think that my son would ever have done this!"

The jury ruled that Mary was mentally ill, and the judge sent her to an asylum. She got out four months later, and moved to France.

By the fall of 1876, Robert Lincoln had three young children and a successful law practice in Chicago. Aside from the fact that his mother refused to speak to him, his life was finally going well.

Then Patrick Tyrrell showed up at his office.

Tyrrell told Robert what he'd learned from Lewis Swegles. Robert was horrified, and urged Tyrrell to protect his father's grave at all costs. Tyrrell promised to do so, assuring him that night guards had already been assigned to patrol the monument grounds.

The next step, Tyrrell said, was to get rid of the guards.

When Robert objected, Tyrrell explained his thinking. The gang at the Hub seemed determined to steal Lincoln's body. Night guards could postpone the attempt, but probably not forever. The only way to end the danger once and for all would be to lure the criminals into the monument—and catch them in the act.

Robert didn't like this at all. But he trusted Tyrrell, and gave his permission. Word was sent to Power in Springfield. The night guards were sent home.

Tyrrell was taking charge of the case—though, technically, he wasn't supposed to. As a Secret Service operative, his job was to disrupt the distribution of counterfeit money. Nobody told him to chase body snatchers.

In his update to Chief Brooks that night, Tyrrell asked for guidance. "Chief, I do not know your views of what my actions should be in a matter not exactly a counterfeiting case, yet they are well represented in this matter. But Sir, I consider it of National Importance, should such an attempt be made, and there should be a National Hanging Bee for those who make the attempt. I shall await your instructions, and be governed thereby."

Brooks got the telegram, read it, and set it aside. He thought Tyrrell was overreacting to wild rumors that probably amounted to nothing.

Tyrrell tried to focus on other cases while awaiting word from Washington. Swegles, meanwhile, returned to the Hub for a series of backroom meetings with Hughes and Mullen.

"Everything was gone over carefully," Swegles later said of his strategy sessions at the Hub, "and the conclusion reached that there were no chances of detection at all. There were no guards at the monument, and all there was to do was to go there, shoulder the casket, and carry it off."

During one of these meetings, Herbert Nelson showed up to brief the team on the Lincoln Monument layout—to help the team, he'd agreed to go to Springfield and take a look, acting like just another tourist. "It's a terribly solid-looking pile," Nelson said of the monument. But there were really only two serious obstacles: the steel door of the tomb chamber, and the heavy marble sarcophagus enclosing Lincoln's casket.

"Hughes and Mullen are very good burglars," Swegles later explained, "although not capable of any work beyond an ordinary house-breaker." They were going to have to go through metal and stone. This would require special tools, maybe even explosives to blast open the marble box.

"You want a man of talent," Swegles told the gang, "someone who's specialized in that sort of work."

What they needed, said Swegles, was a quality cracksman. The others agreed.

Swegles was ready with his suggestion: none other than Billy Brown.

Swegles was used to making it up as he went along. No one told him to encourage the team to bring in a fourth man. But he sensed that they were going in that direction, and he decided he'd feel safer if the fourth man was someone he knew.

Billy Brown was the man he'd supposedly teamed up with to rob the Wisconsin tannery. Actually, no such robbery had occurred. The man Swegles called Billy Brown was really a law-abiding bricklayer, and friend, named Bill Neely.

"He is straight, and I knew he could be trusted," Swegles later said of his choice. What made Brown perfect was his fluency in rough street language. "He can talk crooked," explained Swegles. "He had driven a hack and learned all the slang."

Swegles told Brown he was working for the Secret Service, and assured his friend that he too could make a bit of money as a roper. He persuaded Brown to agree to play a cracksman, then talked Tyrrell into putting Brown on the Secret Service payroll. Tyrrell didn't mind the idea of having another man inside the gang.

Next step: sell Brown to Hughes and Mullen.

"I took Hughes down to my house," Swegles remembered, "and gave him an introduction to Brown, and Hughes took him up to the Hub for the purpose of showing him up to Mullen; and they became satisfied that he was alright. He knew just what he was to do, as I had given him instructions."

Convinced Brown was a skilled crook, the coney men started asking his advice about getting into Lincoln's marble sarcophagus.

"A hole could be drilled in it," Brown told them, "and powder put in and fused, and the whole thing blown to pieces."

Mullen and Hughes were satisfied. Brown helped the gang gather the necessary tools—saws, files, drills, gunpowder, and about six feet of fuse.

Everyone was starting to feel very confident.

Chapter 9
LAST DETAILS

Tyrrell kept sending daily reports to Chief Brooks—and kept waiting for a response.

On October 31 he wrote, "Swegles informs me this day that two men of the gang to remove the remains of President Lincoln are to visit the Monument grounds this week and arrange their plans, and bring them to a close at an early day." The rising tension comes through in Tyrrell's written words. "I have no instructions on this matter, what to do or how to act. Please inform me soon as possible, shall I act or not?"

The next day, still no word from the chief.

Meanwhile, the plot was moving forward. "This morning at ten o'clock," Tyrrell reported, "I met Lewis C. Swegles, who informs me that the gang are consulting on the best means to evade detection after they remove President

Lincoln's remains from the Monument in Springfield."

The plan, Swegles told Tyrrell, was for him and Billy Brown to head north and slip across the border into Canada. "We were to remain there and to be supplied with money to pay our expenses," said Swegles. Hughes and Mullen would come back to Chicago and lie low while Kennally negotiated for the return of Lincoln.

Swegles gave Tyrrell one additional fact, a strange one: "The party intends that Mrs. Boyd will pay all expenses."

Turns out Hughes and Mullen were having trouble pulling together the cash they'd need for travel expenses. "They had been out of coney for some time, and couldn't raise much money," Swegles recalled. It occurred to them that the whole point of this job was to free Ben Boyd. So they decided to hit up his wife, Allie, who was living in Chicago.

They met with her, and made their pitch. She told them she wanted nothing to do with the plot, and insisted they leave her husband out of their wacky-sounding scheme. Allie Boyd did not think her husband would approve. In fact, Ben Boyd was sitting in prison without any idea of the elaborate efforts being made to win his freedom!

Still, Tyrrell waited.

"Chief, I wish you would inform me what action I shall take in this Lincoln Monument matter," he wrote on November 2. If Tyrrell was going to foil the Lincoln plot, he needed the go-ahead. Also, he needed permission to spend a little extra money on train fare and hotels. "It will be attended with considerable expense, which I will not incur without your authority."

That same day Brooks finally replied, though he still didn't take the plot too seriously. "Go ahead," he told Tyrrell, "try to get to the bottom of things."

Late that night, Swegles, Hughes, Mullen, and Billy Brown met at the Hub to review the plan. At some point Mullen ran out to a newsstand and picked up a copy of the *Catholic Union and Times*, a London newspaper. Back at the saloon, he pulled off the front page of the paper and tore it in two, diagonally. He stepped behind the bar, lifted the bust of Abraham Lincoln from its shelf, and shoved one half of the paper into the hollow plaster head. This half would stay hidden in the Hub. The other half he stuffed into his pocket, to take along on the job—and leave in Lincoln's tomb.

This was all part of Big Jim's plot. At the site of the Lincoln job, the police would find half of the front page of the *Catholic Union and Times*. When Big Jim Kennally approached government officials to negotiate for the return of Lincoln's body, they'd demand evidence that Kennally really had the body. Kennally could produce the other half of the newspaper, the one hidden in the Hub. Its ripped edges would fit perfectly together with the half left in Lincoln's tomb. "That would give him some standing with the government officials," Swegles explained—it would prove Kennally was in close touch with the body snatchers.

The Hub gang was convinced there would be no other evidence linking them to the crime.

"Oh, what a desperate undertaking!" Tyrrell wrote in his report to Brooks. "I think Chief, there is no doubt about these people's being in earnest, they really intend to try and accomplish their hellish intentions and thereby gain a

National reputation. It is talked of with a spirit of pride by the man Mullen, he is elated with the prospect of negotiating for the return of President Lincoln's remains, and thereby secure about two hundred thousand dollars and the release of Ben Boyd, for further use, in counterfeiting."

Only one important detail remained—the date of the job. Until Tyrrell knew this, he couldn't set his trap at the monument. And he could only get the information from one place.

On November 5, Tyrrell wrote: "I tried to find Swegles this day but could not."

Swegles was too busy to check in with Tyrrell. He and the Hub gang were holed up in his apartment trying to pick a date for the Lincoln job. They figured about two more weeks would be enough time to get settled in Springfield and take care of last-minute preparations.

"But we talked that over," Swegles recalled, "and came to the conclusion that if we waited so long there would be too much ice, and perhaps snow, and the ground would probably be frozen."

After stealing the body, they'd have to dig a deep hole and plant the casket. Frozen soil would be a major hassle.

"I don't like to dig snow," Hughes grumbled.

Someone suggested election night—November 7, just two days off.

They talked it over, and saw the advantages. The Lincoln Monument would be deserted—everyone would be in town, voting and then waiting for election results to come into the newspaper offices by telegraph. And later that night, as they sped off with Lincoln's casket, the roads would be conveniently busy. "A wagon going along the road at night would not be noticed," Swegles later explained, "since those who saw it would think it contained farmers going home from the polls."

They all agreed—election night it was.

The meeting finally broke up at 2:00 A.M., November 6. The plan was to meet at the Chicago and Alton Depot that night, a few minutes before 9:00, to catch the late train to Springfield.

The morning of November 6 was windy and cold. After just

a few hours of sleep, Swegles found Tyrrell and gave him the update.

Tyrrell told Swegles to go ahead, exactly as if he were really part of the Hub gang. When the thieves got to the monument the next night, Tyrrell would be waiting for them.

The Secret Service spent the day running around Chicago, making final arrangements. At the Palmer House, Tyrrell met with his former boss, Elmer Washburn. Washburn wasn't with the bureau anymore, but he agreed to help out any way he could.

They went to Robert Lincoln's office, told him the latest news, and assured him that his father's remains would not be disturbed. Robert agreed to telegraph John Stuart, chairman of the Lincoln Monument Association, asking him to meet Tyrrell in Springfield the next morning.

"Knowing that there was four persons in the gang," Tyrrell reported, "I needed more help." So Tyrrell and Washburn hurried to the offices of the Pinkerton National Detective Agency and met with the founder, Allan Pinkerton. Pinkerton loaned the Secret Service two of his best private eyes, John McGinn and George Hay.

Tyrrell next dashed off a telegram to John McDonald, the Secret Service agent who'd helped him collar Ben Boyd the year before. McDonald was working in Joliet—Tyrrell told him to get on a train for Springfield.

He also found time to send an update to Washington. It's clear from Tyrrell's wording that his boss *still* wasn't convinced the Lincoln plot was real.

"You think, as I did, that there was no human being so foul as to conceive such a horrible and damnable an act," Tyrrell wrote to Chief Brooks. "But Sir, I am sorry to say that there is."

Chapter 10
OVERNIGHT TRAIN

When Tyrrell, Washburn, and the two private detectives met at the Palmer House that night, the wide street in front of the hotel was lit by the dancing flames of torches. A large group marched past holding torches high, shouting the name of their candidate for president, Samuel J. Tilden.

On a nearby street another huge crowd bellowed the name of their man, Rutherford B. Hayes.

A little after 8:00 P.M., Tyrrell and his team climbed into a wagon and drove toward the train station. Along the way, as arranged, Swegles jumped in for a quick consultation. Everything was on schedule, he told Tyrrell. The Hub gang would meet at the station and take the 9:00 train, riding the first car. Tyrrell handed Swegles fifteen dollars. Swegles jumped out and hurried toward the station on foot.

The detective John McGinn waited a moment, then leaped out and followed the roper down the dark street. "I requested Mr. McGinn to pipe Swegles," reported Tyrrell, "and note the people he would consult with and see where they would go." A smart precaution—Tyrrell could not allow Hughes and Mullen to slip out of sight now.

The wagon continued to the station. Passengers were already boarding the Springfield train. Tyrrell walked into the shadows near the door of the rear car, and waited. He checked his watch: a few minutes before nine. He eyed the platform. Five minutes passed. Steel wheels groaned and clanked against the tracks as the train slowly started rolling.

Tyrrell must have felt a flash of panic—had Swegles been wrong? Misled him? Were the coney men already a step ahead?

Then he spotted a small group darting toward the moving train. Mullen, Hughes, Swegles, and Billy Brown jumped onto the front passenger car.

Tyrrell and the private detectives leaped up the steps of the back car. They found seats and settled in for the two-hundred-mile ride to Springfield. It was not a restful journey.

"With those fiends aboard," Tyrrell jotted in his notebook, "actions may end in death. I fully realize the importance of our journey, Chief, and rest assured Sir, we will do our whole duty."

Mullen sat in the front car, a big bag of tools between his feet. Hughes sat beside him. Swegles suggested that maybe they shouldn't all ride together.

"Four men together might prove singular," he said—too memorable to potential witnesses, if things went wrong. He

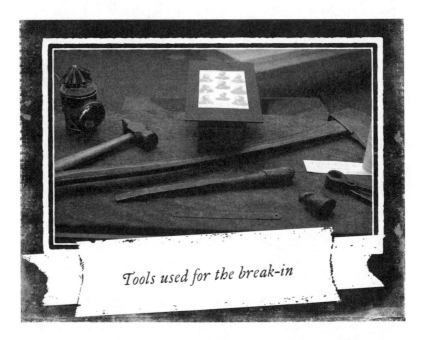

Tools used for the break-in

and Brown walked back to the next car.

This was a little detail worked out between the roper and his friend. Billy Brown had absolutely no intention of going to Springfield and getting mixed up in the tomb break-in. When the train slowed down to pass through Burlington, he jumped off. From the side of the tracks, Brown watched the red light hanging from the caboose shrink and vanish.

He headed back toward Chicago, and once again became Bill Neely, the law-abiding bricklayer.

Swegles strolled to the front car and reported that the cracksman was sound asleep.

The train pulled into Springfield at 6:00 A.M. on November 7. It was still dark, and an icy wind whipped through the station.

Hughes stepped onto the platform and pulled his blue overcoat around him. Mullen followed wrapped in a long raincoat, carrying his heavy bag. Swegles told them Billy Brown was still in the next car, sleeping. He said he'd go wake the cracksman before the train left the station at 7:00 A.M.

The three men walked into town, found a restaurant that was open early, and ordered breakfast. When they stepped back outside, the sky was beginning to lighten from black to wet gray. They walked through town, toward a saloon called the Germania House. Mullen held up the bag full of tools.

"He handed them to me," Swegles later said, "and told me to take them into a lager-beer saloon, and say to the bartender that my friend wasn't up, and ask him to keep the bag until I called for it." The two coney men preferred not to be seen with the tools, given what they were about to be used for. Of course Swegles knew he was being taken advantage of— but he was pretty sure he'd get the last laugh.

When Swegles came back out, the men walked to the St. Charles House, a small hotel. "They were very tired," remembered Swegles. "I told them I would go downtown and wake Brown."

Mullen said, "You had better let him go to one of the towns four or five miles out, and hire a rig."

Swegles agreed. The plan was to have Brown bring a wagon to the cemetery that night, for the getaway.

Mullen and Hughes entered the hotel and registered as "T. Durnan and James Smith." Mullen asked the manager to wake them at 10:30 A.M., and they went up to their room.

If the coney men were watching from the window, they saw their partner walking in the direction of the train station. When Swegles was a few blocks from the hotel, well out of view, he doubled back toward the St. Nicholas Hotel, just two blocks from the St. Charles. He went in and asked the clerk for the room number of a guest named "Mr. Demorest."

Chapter 11

ELECTION DAY

It was a cold, overcast morning in Springfield. A steady stream of wagons rolled into town, packed with men coming in to vote. Shop owners swept the sidewalks in front of their stores and arranged displays, expecting a busy day.

Patrick Tyrrell, registered as C. A. Demorest, sat in his room in the St. Nicholas Hotel. Swegles ducked in, gave his update, and left. At about 9:00 A.M., John Stuart, chairman of the Lincoln Monument Association, came in. Tyrrell briefed Stuart on the plot, and his plans to bust it up. Together they rode in Stuart's carriage out to Oak Ridge Cemetery.

John Carroll Power was at the monument that morning, greeting visitors as always. Stuart introduced Power to Tyrrell and told him to do whatever the Secret Service operative asked. Knowing of the earlier attempt to steal

Lincoln, Power was probably not shocked by the news that another try would be made that night.

"Tyrrell and I then made a thorough examination of the grounds and of the interior of the Monument," Power recalled. He showed Tyrrell Memorial Hall, and then they walked around the monument to the doors in front of the catacomb. The wooden door was open, allowing Tyrrell to step up to the iron gate. Through the bars he could see Lincoln's sarcophagus on the floor of the small room.

Tyrrell looked at the brick wall at the back of the room. He asked Power what was behind it.

A sort of labyrinth, Power explained—a series of thick walls holding up the massive obelisk above, with narrow, mazelike passages between the walls.

Tyrrell asked to take a look. They went back around the monument and through Memorial Hall. Power lit a lantern and led Tyrrell into the labyrinth. The air inside was thick with cold moisture and the stink of rotting wood. Water seeped through the stones above, dripping on the men, pooling on the muddy floor. Tyrrell followed Power past piles of lumber left behind by workmen, turning right, then

Lincoln's tomb at Oak Ridge Cemetery

left, then left again. At a brick wall that looked to Tyrrell like any other in the maze, Power stopped. This was the wall they had just seen from the other side, Power said— behind it was the catacomb, and Lincoln's tomb.

Tyrrell suggested an experiment. He waited by the wall while Power walked out of the labyrinth and around to the catacomb. Power unlocked the iron door, entered, and rapped his knuckles against Lincoln's marble sarcophagus. Tyrrell heard the sound through the brick wall. Just what he wanted to know.

They met outside. Tyrrell told Power that most likely the men planning the robbery would visit the monument during the day. "He gave a description of them," Power remembered, "and instructed me to show them everything usually shown to visitors, and to answer truthfully all questions."

Tyrrell said he'd be back early that evening. He asked Power to stick around at least until then.

At about 11:00 A.M., Swegles walked into the St. Charles hotel.

"They were up," Swegles later said of Hughes and Mullen.

"I told them that Brown had gone." The cracksman was in the next town, Swegles explained, arranging the wagon. If none were available for rent, he'd steal one. A perfectly credible story. "For we knew," Swegles said, "there would be lots of them hitched all over town, belonging to men who had come in to see how the election was going."

Swegles left the hotel. A bit later, Hughes and Mullen came out and strolled the busy downtown streets. Rowdy crowds were gathering outside voting places. Gamblers were taking bets on the election. The coney men felt safe among all this excitement, knowing no one would remember seeing them.

The men killed some time in a saloon, then stopped in a shoe shop and waited while the shoemaker patched a hole in Hughes's shoe. They met Swegles again early in the afternoon. Time to go check out the monument, Mullen said.

"He suggested that Hughes and I go up to the cemetery and take a look at the tomb," recalled Swegles. "He said he might be noticed at the tomb, as his black mustache looked a little crooked, and he resembled a sporting man. His object was to save himself from being identified."

Wasn't Mullen worried about witnesses seeing his

partners' faces at what was about to become the crime scene? Evidently not.

At about 2:30 P.M., Swegles and Hughes got on a streetcar for the twenty-minute ride to Oak Ridge Cemetery. They didn't notice two men jump on behind them.

"I sent McGinn and Hay to pipe them," Tyrrell reported.

"Near three o'clock two men appeared answering the description given by Tyrrell," John Carroll Power remembered. They paid the gatekeeper the twenty-five-cent admission fee, walked up the dirt path leading to the Lincoln Monument, and introduced themselves to Power as Lewis and Smith, of Wisconsin.

As Power showed them around, the visitors had a lot of questions. "I answered all their questions truly and without hesitation," said the custodian.

The men rode back to town, found Mullen in his hotel room, and shared the good news. They had gotten a decent look at the marble box holding Lincoln, and it didn't look as thick as Nelson had led them to believe. It could be lifted, Hughes said, or easily smashed.

"Why, I could pick it open," he bragged. "I could fall against it and open it."

Swegles explained what they'd learned from Power about the wooden and lead caskets inside the marble sarcophagus.

"We'll break it open," Mullen said of the marble. "We might as well have an axe, because we may have to open the inside."

Mullen pulled out a very long, empty sack. The plan was to lift the casket into their wagon—the sack was plan B. "In case the casket was too heavy for us," Swegles later explained, "the intention was to break it open, double the body up, and put it in the bag."

Next they spread out a map of Sangamon County. Mullen pointed to a bridge over the Sangamon River, about two miles out of town.

"We will take it up there and dump the casket into the water," Mullen said. "The casket will go to the bottom, and no one will ever think of looking for it there." If the water wasn't deep enough to hide the casket, Mullen suggested, they'd bury it under the bridge. Either way, the wagon and team would wait on the stone bridge. Horses leave obvious tracks when they stand still on a dirt road, but this wouldn't be a problem on stone. The roads themselves would be so crisscrossed with wagon tracks, theirs could never be spotted.

The bridge plan was a major break from Big Jim's instructions—what happened to driving the body to the Indiana sand dunes? Mullen must have decided against the long trip. Stashing Lincoln two miles out of Springfield had its risks, but it beat a two-hundred-and-twenty-mile drive with the body in the back of their wagon.

Mullen had one more surprise in store for Swegles.

"If we can get $10,000 or $15,000 more, as well as a pardon for Boyd, would you be willing to stay in jail for a year?"

Mullen explained his thinking. After the job, Swegles would be tucked away safely in Canada. But what if authorities refused to pay the ransom unless they were given at least one of the grave robbers? In that case, Swegles would have to take the fall.

Mullen assured Swegles he'd be well taken care of in his prison cell.

Swegles agreed to the last-second change.

"It got along toward dark," Swegles recalled. "Hughes and Mullen went to get supper." Swegles said he'd go check on Billy Brown.

A few minutes later he knocked on Tyrrell's door at the St. Nicholas. Detectives McGinn and Hay were there. Swegles shared the latest news, and said the plan was to leave for the cemetery at 8:30 P.M.

While they were talking, Elmer Washburn showed up, along with Secret Service agent John McDonald, and a third man. Washburn introduced the stranger as John English, a reporter from the *Chicago Tribune*. Somehow English had picked up rumors of something serious brewing in Springfield, and he'd run into Washburn on the train to town. Washburn agreed to bring him along for the showdown. This must have annoyed Tyrrell, but English would later write the most detailed eyewitness account of the events of the next few hours.

Tyrrell went over his plan one last time for the small crowd. He and the other cops would already be in Memorial Hall when the grave robbers arrived. Swegles was to wait until Hughes and Mullen had begun trying to open the marble sarcophagus. Then Swegles would slip out, hurry to the door of Memorial Hall, and whisper the password: "Wash"—Washburn's nickname. If, for any reason, he couldn't get close enough to be heard in a whisper, he should stand in view of the door and light a cigar.

At that point, Tyrrell explained, the lawmen would catch the grave robbers red-handed.

The detectives all pulled out their pistols, checked to make sure they were loaded and ready. Swegles left to find Hughes and Mullen. A few minutes later, just after dark, Tyrrell's team climbed into a wagon and headed for the monument.

Chapter 12
NIGHT AT THE MONUMENT

The coney men were still at dinner at the St. Charles, with loaded pistols stuck in their pockets.

Swegles took a seat and told his partners he'd found Billy Brown at a hotel across town. Brown had picked up what Swegles described as a "rattling good pair of bay horses and a three-spring wagon." As soon as Swegles grabbed a bite to eat, he explained, he'd hurry back to Brown and have him come pick them all up.

"Don't have him do that!" Mullen gasped. "I thought you had more sense."

Swegles fought the urge to smile. He knew Mullen would react that way, or he'd never have dared suggest he could deliver a wagon that didn't actually exist.

"Go to him, and have him keep away," ordered Mullen.

Tell him to drive out to the cemetery at 9:30 P.M., Mullen said, and tie up his team in the woods. Tell him to tiptoe up to the monument and give a quiet whistle near the door of the tomb chamber.

Swegles agreed.

"I went off and got some oysters," he recalled. He lingered over the meal, allowing enough time to pass to make it believable that he'd walked back and forth across town. Then he met his partners near the train station.

"How is it?" Mullen whispered.

"All right," Swegles said. He'd seen Brown, given him Mullen's instructions.

Mullen still seemed nervous. "Does he understand perfectly about going up with the team?"

"Yes."

"Let's get ready and go."

Swegles walked into the Germania House and asked the bartender for his bag of tools. He came out with the bag and they started walking. Behind a building in town, Mullen spotted an axe leaning on a woodpile. He picked it up. They followed the streetcar tracks down the dark road out of town.

John Carroll Power was still on duty at the Lincoln Monument.

"The sun had not been visible during the whole of the day," he remembered, "and thick clouds hung like a pall over the earth, making it so dark as early as six o'clock that a man could scarcely have seen his hand before him."

Tyrrell and his men jumped out of the wagon in front of the path leading up to the monument. Tyrrell paid the hack driver and told him to turn around and drive right back to town—just to make sure that when the coney men arrived, they wouldn't see anyone near the monument.

The team walked up the hill to Memorial Hall. Power let them in and locked the doors behind them. "Inside Memorial Hall the darkness could almost be felt," he recalled.

"It was deemed advisable to remain in this room," explained John English, the *Chicago Tribune* reporter. "If the officers were scattered around the monument, lying among the bush, the thieves were liable to step on them."

Power picked up some matches and a lantern, and asked the other men to link hands. Holding the unlit lamp in one hand and Tyrrell's hand in the other, Power led the way into the narrow halls of the labyrinth beneath the monument. The group snaked around several corners, reaching a spot from which no light could escape to the outside. Power struck a match and lit the lantern. He handed it to Tyrrell, who continued through the maze to the brick wall separating the labyrinth from Lincoln's tomb chamber.

Tyrrell told John English to stand in this spot, and listen. The reporter thought he was there to get a story, but Tyrrell was putting him to work. Sounds made in the chamber could be heard here in the labyrinth, Tyrrell explained.

"Imperative silence was demanded," English recalled. "The slightest movement produced an echo which might give an alarm."

Next, Tyrrell lit a series of lamps and placed them along the damp dirt floor of the labyrinth, lighting the way from the back wall most of the way to Memorial Hall. When English heard men at work in the catacomb, he was to follow the lamps out of the maze, and report to Tyrrell.

"Each man was assigned his post," Tyrrell explained. He pointed Power and the detectives to dark edges of the Hall, and took the front post himself. "I was stationed at the outside door of Memorial Hall, to communicate with Swegles."

As the men found their spots, the clap of shoe soles on marble seemed to echo like thunder.

"Take off your boots," Tyrrell said, "and keep quiet."

He slipped off his own shoes. The men waited in their socks, in silence, in the dark. Time seemed to pass very slowly, but there was no way to know for sure.

"It was not possible for us to consult our watches without danger of revealing our presence to the thieves," Power said.

Mullen, Hughes, and Swegles got to the cemetery about two hours after Tyrrell's crew. Everything looked good—dark and silent. Still, to be extra sure they weren't seen, the men walked past the main gate and climbed over the cemetery fence at a spot far from the road.

They snuck to the bottom of the hill on which the

monument stood. Swegles set down the tool bag and pulled out a bull's-eye lantern. These were the flashlights of their day—the sides of the lantern were solid metal, with just one small glass window for light to stream out in a narrow beam.

"Let's go on and take a look around," whispered Swegles, picking up the axe.

Mullen lit the lantern wick and gestured toward the monument. "Is there a bed in there a man would be liable to sleep on?"

"I guess not," Swegles said, "but the old man might be in there reading or writing. Come on," he said to Hughes, "you and I will go around there."

"Hurry up," Mullen said, "and give me the signal if there is anything wrong."

Swegles and Hughes headed up the hill with the lantern. If anything didn't look right, they were to whistle to Mullen.

They walked around the dark monument to the door of Memorial Hall. Swegles grabbed the door handle and shook it. Locked.

Inside, Tyrrell flattened himself against the wall beside the door.

Swegles lifted the bull's-eye and pointed a shaft of light right through the door window. "I flashed the light in, but saw nothing," Swegles later said. "I didn't of course want to see anything."

Swegles told Hughes it was clear. Hughes stepped up to the door and had a look for himself.

Then they walked around the monument toward the catacomb doors.

Tyrrell gestured for Power to unlock the door of Memorial Hall. Power put in his key and turned it, but left the door closed.

On the opposite side of the monument, Mullen pried open the outer, wooden door leading to the catacomb.

"How is it?" he asked when Swegles and Hughes walked up.

The two men confirmed they saw no one.

Mullen reached into the bag, took out a hacksaw, and went to work on the thick padlock securing the inner iron gate. It was slow going, and Mullen spat curses as he dragged the blade back and forth.

This was going to take a while, Swegles saw. "I'll make a check," he said, and walked around to the other side of the monument.

Only 150 feet from where Mullen was working, Tyrrell watched and listened from his spot near the door of Memorial Hall.

"Wash."

Tyrrell heard the password. He pushed the door open a crack.

Swegles stepped forward. In quick, whispered words, he told Tyrrell that Mullen and Hughes were sawing the lock.

Tyrrell told Swegles to go back and help them. He wasn't ready to pounce yet—not until the thieves could be nabbed actually handling the tomb.

Swegles walked back to the catacomb door. Hughes had his hands around the padlock, holding it steady while Mullen worked the saw. They were about a third of the way through when the blade suddenly snapped.

"A splendid saw!" Mullen muttered.

He threw down the broken tool and reached into the bag.

"They then got a three-cornered file," Swegles said, "and

Hughes held the lock while Mullen filed. They took turns at it. It was very hard and slow work."

When Mullen had filed about halfway through the lock, he took out a pair of pliers and grabbed the lock, yanking and twisting until the metal finally cracked. The broken lock fell to the ground.

Mullen pushed the gate open and entered the small room. Hughes stepped in with the lantern, followed by Swegles.

Hughes pointed the light at the floor. There it was: the long, white marble sarcophagus. At one end, carved into the stone, was the name: LINCOLN. In an arc above the name were the famous words of his second inaugural address: WITH MALICE TOWARD NONE, WITH CHARITY FOR ALL.

Hughes and Mullen crouched beside the marble box, feeling the edges for a weak spot in the construction. Swegles figured this was his chance to slip away. He began backing toward the door.

Mullen told him to wait—he was needed inside.

Hughes held the lantern out to Swegles and told him to stand in the corner, out of sight of the door, aiming a beam of light at the sarcophagus. Swegles glanced at the open door, then back to the coney men. He considered making a run for it, but thought of the pistols in his partners' pockets. He'd played his role perfectly so far; this was no time to panic. He took the lantern.

Mullen couldn't find an easy way into the sarcophagus. He'd have to crack it open, either with his axe or the gunpowder in his bag. He tried the axe first, lifting it above his head, preparing to slam the blunt end down on the marble lid.

"Hold on!" Swegles said.

Mullen stopped.

"If we can get the lid off," suggested Swegles, "we can put it on again and it won't be known that the coffin is gone." Was Swegles really worried about damaging the sarcophagus? Or did he just want the job to take as long as possible, so he'd have time to slip away? He never explained.

Anyway, Mullen agreed to try and pry the thing open. He slid the axe blade under the lid and pushed down on the handle. The lid came right up. He and Swegles lifted the slab off the box and leaned it against the empty crypt reserved for Mary Lincoln. Beneath the top slab was a second, heavier marble lid, cemented to the box below.

They began hacking at the cement seam with the axe and chisels.

Chapter 13
DEVILISH WORK

John English could hear the banging from his spot at the back of the labyrinth. The reporter followed the series of lanterns through the maze and into Memorial Hall.

"They are in the catacomb," he told Tyrrell.

Tyrrell didn't seem to react. Everyone in Memorial Hall now heard the distant clank of metal on marble. They all watched Tyrrell, waiting for him to give the signal to move out.

"Not a man moved," Power remembered. He couldn't figure out what Tyrrell was waiting for, and was becoming increasingly anxious.

Tyrrell waited, and listened. To this point, everything had gone exactly according to his script. Just a few moments more, and the crooks would have their hands on the coffin.

In the catacomb, the men cracked through the cement seal of Lincoln's sarcophagus. All pushing together, they were able to slowly shove the thick slab off the top of the box.

Swegles lifted the bull's-eye, purposely swinging it a bit too wildly—desperately hoping the signal would be seen by someone outside.

"Look out," hissed Mullen. "Be careful!"

Swegles pointed the beam of yellow light into the open sarcophagus. Inside, as they'd been told, was the red cedar coffin.

They quickly cut through the cement holding the panel at the head of the sarcophagus. This allowed them to begin dragging the coffin out of the marble box.

"The casket was then pulled out about a foot," Swegles remembered, "and it was found to weigh not over four hundred to five hundred pounds."

Not as bad as Mullen and Hughes had feared. Three men could handle it, though not for long distances. They'd need the wagon nearby.

Mullen checked his watch: nearly 9:30 P.M. Billy Brown

hadn't given his whistle yet, but Mullen figured he should be getting to his spot in the woods any moment.

"You had better go and see if you can find anything of him," Mullen told Swegles, "and get him to come help carry this." He warned Swegles not to try coming back up the hill to the monument without signaling first. "We are not going to let anyone come monkeying around here."

Mullen and Hughes began gathering the tools as Swegles set down the lantern and ran down the hill, away from the monument. He scurried into a clump of trees at the base of the hill, exactly where Brown was supposed to be hiding with his team of horses and wagon.

"When I got a bunch of woods between them and me," Swegles said, referring to his partners in the catacomb, "I turned sharp to the right, and up toward the road leading to Memorial Hall."

Tyrrell and his team were still waiting inside. They saw a man's figure approaching the door.

"Wash!"

The door squeaked as Tyrrell swung it open.

Swegles give his update: The men had already moved the coffin a foot or so. Just the evidence Tyrrell was waiting for.

"You stay here," Tyrrell told the roper, and signaling to the detectives, he said, "Let's go."

They all drew their pistols and headed out the door. English followed behind to watch. "Up to this time," he would soon write, "everything had worked to a charm—not a mistake had been made."

The moment Tyrrell's feet hit the cold pavement he realized he hadn't put his boots back on. Too late now, he figured. He hurried on in his socks. The others spread out behind him on the grass.

Then suddenly: *BOOM!*—the unmistakable crack and echo of a gunshot. In the silence of the cemetery, it sounded like a volcanic eruption.

Tyrrell turned to the blast. George Hay's pistol was smoking—the thing had accidentally gone off as he ran. The element of surprise was lost.

"Come on!" Tyrrell shouted.

He sprinted around the monument to the catacomb door

and kicked open the unlocked iron gate, pointing his pistol into the dark chamber.

"Come out with your hands up!"

No response.

Tyrrell slid inside, his back flat to the stone wall. His eyes moved uselessly around the tiny space—too dark to see anything.

"One wrong move and you're dead men!"

There was no sound, not even breathing.

Tyrrell pulled out a match and lit it. The room was empty.

"The marks of their Devilish work were plainly visible," he reported. Flaming match in his hand, Tyrrell's eyes darted around the room: a marble slab leaning on the wall, another on the floor, a broken padlock, pieces of a hacksaw blade, a chisel, an axe with marble dust on the blade.

"Search the grounds!" Tyrrell roared to his detectives. "They can't have gone far!"

He ran back outside—and again felt the cold ground through his socks. He dashed around the monument, grabbed his boots, pulled them on, and joined the hunt.

Power stood outside the door of Memorial Hall, looking out at the grounds. "It was now approaching the time for the moon to rise," he recalled. He watched the search in the faint light.

With a cocked pistol in his hand, Tyrrell started up one of the four sets of stairs around the monument. Each staircase led to the terrace surrounding the obelisk, sixteen feet above the ground.

He got to the top of the stairs and stepped onto the terrace. About seventy feet in front of him, a figure darted toward a stone column.

"Halt!" Tyrrell called, lifting his gun.

The figure didn't stop. Tyrrell fired.

The man shot back and disappeared around the corner. Tyrrell chased, and saw two figures duck behind granite pedestals. He fired again. Two bullets screamed back at him and sped past—so close he felt the wind on his cheek.

"Men, come up here!" Tyrrell screamed. "We have the devils up here!"

John McDonald raced up the stairs, shouting, "Men, surround the obelisk!"

An artist's drawing of the tomb chamber

The interior of the tomb's obelisk

There was a short silence.

Then, from behind one of the granite pedestals, a man called: "Tyrrell, is that you?"

Tyrrell didn't answer. He didn't want to give away his position.

"Tyrrell!" the voice called again. "For God's sake, answer! Is that you shooting at us?"

The men peeked out from behind the pedestals. Tyrrell lifted his pistol to fire—and in the light of the rising moon, saw he was aiming at George Hay and John McGinn.

"My God!" gasped Tyrrell. "What a narrow escape!"

"Then the villains are gone," groaned Hay.

And they really were.

Tyrrell later blamed George Hay's accidental gunshot for alerting the body snatchers and allowing them to escape, but he was equally to blame. Why had he waited so long once the men started cracking open the sarcophagus? And why hadn't he stationed anyone outside the monument, to keep watch on the catacomb door?

Let's go back to the moment Swegles left the sarcophagus,

supposedly to go find Billy Brown. Swegles disappeared into the woods, leaving Hughes and Mullen in the tiny room, with Lincoln's coffin at their feet.

Something about the setup made them nervous. It's not that they suspected Swegles of double-dealing. But their crook's instincts told them not to stand around in this enclosed space—they'd be safer waiting outside, where they could spot anyone coming, and where escape routes existed.

Leaving the tools behind, the two men jogged down the hill toward the dark line of trees. They lay on the grass, out of sight, listening and watching. The thin light of the rising moon gave them a dim view of the Lincoln Monument, about one hundred feet away.

Just seconds after they reached their spot, they saw shapes moving, black silhouettes against the monument's gray marble. Swegles and Brown? No, there were too many figures, four or five.

Then came the explosion of Hay's pistol.

At that point, Hughes and Mullen jumped up and darted through the woods toward the nearest fence. They climbed over and started sprinting down the street.

The streetcar from Springfield had just finished its last run of the night. The driver, Charles Elkin, would later tell police he saw two men speeding past, and heard a burst of gunfire—the shoot-out on the monument terrace.

Hughes and Mullen ran until their legs throbbed, then walked, continuing north all night. As the moon rose higher, the sky got brighter. Whenever they heard a wagon approaching, they ducked into a ditch or bushes along the side of the road.

By dawn they were many miles from Springfield.

Back at the monument, Power lit a bunch of lanterns and handed them out to the detectives.

"All were pale and quivering with emotion," he recalled. Seeing the agony in Tyrrell's eyes, Power couldn't help thinking the operative had actually been lucky. "If Tyrrell had found them in the catacomb," noted Power, "entering the door as he did, they could and would have seen and shot him before he could have learned which one of the dark corners they were in."

The entire group walked to the catacomb to inspect the

damage. Power's main concern was Lincoln's coffin—was there any chance it had been opened? He crouched down, holding his light near the wood. There were no cracks, no signs it had been forced open.

Then he examined the screws holding the box together, one by one. The grooves were filled with a flaky layer of orange rust. If anyone had tried to turn the screws, the screwdriver would have chipped the rust.

"The remains up to that time were absolutely safe," Power reported.

All the evidence was left in place. Power slid a new padlock on the iron door and clicked it shut.

The men gathered in Memorial Hall to discuss next steps. Tyrrell suggested that he, McDonald, and Hay take the midnight train back to Chicago. Hughes and Mullen would surface there sooner or later, Tyrrell figured, and with luck they might even be on the train. Washburn and McGinn agreed to stay in Springfield to inspect the grounds by daylight, and question possible witnesses in town.

Then they all walked back to town. It was past 11:00 P.M., but the streets were still brightly lit and crowded. People stood outside newspaper offices, waiting for election results to come in from around the country.

English wrote up a quick story on the monument break-in and telegraphed it to the *Tribune* offices in Chicago. Washburn sent a much shorter wire to Robert Lincoln:

"Parties escaped. Temporarily baffled but confident of arrest soon."

As the overnight train rolled out of Springfield, Tyrrell walked through every car, inspecting faces. Hughes and Mullen were not aboard.

Swegles was, but he was careful to avoid eye contact with the operative. It was important the two not be seen together—just in case any of the coney men's friends happened to be aboard. But at some point in the middle of the night, Tyrrell risked a quick consultation with the roper. He slipped Swegles ten dollars and asked if he'd be willing to help hunt Hughes and Mullen. Swegles agreed.

When the train pulled into Chicago early that morning, Swegles headed home and Tyrrell went to his office to write up his report to Chief Brooks. "I have now, sir, given you the details of one of the most unfortunate nights I ever have experienced," he concluded. "The encounter on President Lincoln's monument shall ever be remembered by me."

Tyrrell confessed he had no idea where the suspects were, adding, "But, Chief, their capture is only a question of time."

As an exhausted Tyrrell hunched over his office desk in Chicago, Hughes and Mullen trudged on through the chilly morning somewhere near the town of Sherman, Illinois. By 8:00 A.M., they were drained, filthy, starving, and hopelessly lost. When they saw two farmers loading sacks of potatoes into a wagon, they took a chance.

"Seen any strangers around here?" Hughes called out.

The farmers, John Dixon and Thomas Keagle, looked up from their work. As they later told newspapers, they were instantly wary of these dusty travelers.

"Why?" asked Keagle.

"There was a row in Springfield last night," Hughes said, pitching the story he and Mullen had concocted to explain their tired eyes and dirty clothes. A man had been stabbed, Hughes explained, and he and Mullen were out looking for the killers.

The farmers were unconvinced. Why, they asked Hughes, had he and his friend chosen to chase a bunch of murderers on foot?

Hughes mumbled something about having left his wagon back by the river.

Mullen jumped in with the real reason they'd stopped, asking if the men might spare some milk, maybe a bite of bread.

No, said the farmers.

Well, Mullen asked, could they at least point out the direction to the nearest train station?

The farmers did this, and Hughes and Mullen headed east.

Turning back to their potatoes, the farmers discussed the strange encounter. The hungry strangers appeared to be on the run, they agreed, and were probably criminals of some kind. Keagle wanted to go grab them, or at least tell someone in town. Dixon just wanted to get back to work. They decided to go back to work.

The two farmers would have been even more suspicious if

they had read that morning's *Chicago Tribune*.

Election news dominated the first few pages. Results in a few states were still unclear, but the *Tribune* was ready to make its call. "When we write these lines all the indications are that Samuel. J. Tilden has been elected President of the United States."

Not until readers reached page five did they see a story from Springfield, with this headline: "Dastardly Attempt to Despoil the Lincoln Monument: Thieves Trying to Steal the Bones of the Martyr President."

This was the short article John English had telegraphed to Chicago the night before. He briefly described the tomb break-in and the narrow escape of the body snatchers. "If human ingenuity can track them it will be done," he stated. "It is earnestly hoped that the double-distilled perpetrators of this attempted robbery of the remains of America's most loved President will soon be brought to justice."

Later that morning, English watched Washburn and McGinn search the Lincoln Monument grounds for clues. Beneath a tree they found the bull's-eye lantern, its glass lens cracked. Nearby they found a patch of grass with its green blades pressed flat against the dirt—two men had been lying there very recently. From this spot, two sets of footprints led to the fence and out to the street.

While the detectives gathered evidence, a steady stream of visitors walked up to the monument to see the crime scene for themselves. John Carroll Power patiently answered questions, as always. Yes, there had been a break-in. No, the thieves had not taken Lincoln's body. And no, visitors could not see the catacomb. Both doors to the tomb chamber remained closed and locked.

Inside, sticking more than a foot out of its broken marble box, Lincoln's coffin rested on the tile floor.

At 10:30 that morning, a still-sleepless Tyrrell checked in with Robert Lincoln.

"Mr. Lincoln expressed his satisfaction and asked if I could arrest the parties Mullen and Hughes," Tyrrell recalled. "I told him that it was only a question of time, that in a few days they would both show up."

Tyrrell didn't know that for sure, of course. But his long experience as a cop told him that crooks almost always drift back to their friends, their home base, the place they feel safe. It's one of the main reasons criminals get caught. With this in mind, he met Swegles and asked his roper to return to the Hub.

"But act very cautious," he added.

This was a dicey assignment for Swegles. It was a safe bet Big Jim had read that morning's *Tribune*. He'd surely be fuming about the fiasco in Springfield—and very eager to know how the police had just happened to be there. Still, it would be even *more* dangerous for Swegles to stay away from the Hub. Avoiding it would make him look like he had something to hide.

Early the next morning, November 9, Hughes and Mullen reached the railroad station at Chestnut, about forty miles northeast of Springfield. They had no money for tickets, but when a train pulled in, they jumped on.

When the conductor came around to collect tickets, Hughes was ready with another half-baked story. He and his friend had just bought a bunch of cattle, and blown all their cash. Hughes did not attempt to explain where the cows were at the moment, or why buying livestock should get him out of paying for his train ticket.

Instead he pulled out his revolver and offered to let the conductor hold on to it until they got to the town of Melvin. There, he'd get cash from his family, pay for the tickets, and take back his gun. The conductor stuck the pistol in his pocket—it was worth a lot more than two train tickets.

Hughes and Mullen hopped off in Melvin and walked to Hughes's father's nearby farm. He told his dad he and Mullen had been in Texas, borrowed a few dollars, went back to the station, paid for the tickets, and picked up his gun. Then Hughes returned to his father's place to lie low, rest, and eat.

Mullen was worried about his saloon and eager to talk to Swegles. He got on the next train and headed to Chicago.

Back in Springfield, Lincoln still lay on the floor.

Power begged for help from John Stuart of the Monument Association, and Stuart agreed to send out Adam Johnston, a Springfield marble dealer. As Power looked on, Johnston and two of his employees shoved the coffin back into the sarcophagus. They cemented the top and front pieces back on.

A few days later, Stuart rode out to the monument himself. He was too worried to sleep at night, he told Power. They'd fixed the marble box, but so what? Lincoln's body was right back where it had been when the thieves almost made off with it. Something more had to be done.

Johnston and his workmen returned. Power let them into the catacomb, and the marble workers cracked open the sarcophagus. They pulled out Lincoln's coffin and dragged it to a dark corner, where it could not be seen from outside. Then they carefully sealed up the sarcophagus and left it in its usual spot in the middle of the room.

Johnston came back after dark, this time without his workers. Power was there, as arranged. So were John Stuart and two other members of the association.

"We five then carried the coffin from the catacomb, around the east side of the monument, to Memorial Hall," Power recalled. Their arms and shoulders burning with pain, the men hurried through the hall, into the dark labyrinth, twisted around a few turns, and set the five-hundred-pound

Lincoln's coffin, hidden inside the foundations of the monument

box down by the base of the obelisk.

Worn-out and aching, Stuart and his friends headed home. Johnson and Power carried wooden planks through the labyrinth and started hammering together a huge box, building it right around Lincoln's cedar coffin. "It was exceedingly hard work for two men," Power said, "and the atmosphere we had to breathe was almost stifling for want of ventilation."

The job finally done, Power thanked Johnston and sent him home. He did not want anyone to see what he was going to do next.

Chapter 15
BACK TO THE HUB

On November 10, Patrick Tyrrell picked up the morning newspapers and sat down to read.

It was three days since the election and both candidates were claiming victory. Based on the states he'd won, Tilden had a total of 184 electoral votes; Hayes had 166. Results in three states—Florida, South Carolina, and Louisiana—were still too close to call. These states had a total of 19 electoral votes, so if Hayes won all three he'd have a 185–184 victory. Of course, he believed he *had* won all three. Tilden begged to differ. While local election boards recounted ballots, Democrats and Republicans traded charges of fraud and threats of legal action.

Buried beneath the election articles were a few updates on the Lincoln grave robbing plot. The *Tribune*, with its eyewitness reporter, had the most accurate information. Other papers either ignored the bizarre story, or called it a hoax. "What could anyone want with the bones of Lincoln?" mocked the *Tribune*'s rival paper, the *Chicago Times*.

Critics also complained about the detective work involved. If Tyrrell had really been there at the monument, waiting for break-in, how had he managed to let the crooks slip away?

The Lincoln story even became part of the raging election controversy. Republicans suggested that Democrats had tried to steal Lincoln's corpse as revenge for defeating the South in the Civil War. Democrats fired back that Republicans staged the crime themselves—to make people think it had been done by Democrats!

None of this did anything to improve Tyrrell's mood.

Then, tucked away on the crime page of one of the papers, was an item of interest. Two men had been caught for burglary in Lincoln, about forty miles from Springfield. Tyrrell raced to the telegraph office and fired off a note to the Lincoln city marshal:

"Please telegraph me a quick description of the men arrested in your town for robbing Mr. Sherman's house. Are they still locked up?"

The description came back—not a match.

Tyrrell had no solid leads. Between the strain of the past week and the pressure of the ongoing mystery, the detective's strong body was wearing down. "Taken very sick with pains and fever," he wrote that night.

Then he went home and collapsed into bed.

Lewis Swegles scurried through the alley behind the Hub, pushed open the back door, and peered in. Big Jim Kennally stood behind the bar, serving drinks. Above him, on its little shelf, sat the plaster bust of Abraham Lincoln.

Swegles motioned to a friend inside, asking him to let Kennally know he was there. He was a wanted man, as far as Kennally knew, and he needed to act like one.

Kennally stepped out into the dark alley, seething.

"You boys are a pack of fools and babies!" he hissed at Swegles. "You should be spanked and put to bed!"

Between curses, Kennally told Swegles he hadn't heard

from Hughes and Mullen, had no idea where they were—and hoped to never see them again.

The conversation was over.

Actually, Mullen was already in Chicago, lying low. He got in touch with a friend and asked her to bring a question to Swegles—was the coast clear? The woman found Swegles and delivered the message.

"The thing is all right," Swegles told her. The papers were caught up with the election, and treating the Lincoln story like a joke. There was no heat at all from the Secret Service or police.

The next day, November 11, Mullen was back behind the bar at the Hub.

"Being very sick this day, unable to get out of bed," Tyrrell scrawled in his daily report.

But he must have at least sat up when Swegles charged in with the news about Mullen. Swegles explained that he hadn't spoken with Mullen yet, but planned to meet him that night. And there was news from Hughes, too: he was holed up at his father's farm, about one hundred miles from Chicago.

"I instructed Swegles to be very anxious about them," Tyrrell reported, "and paid him five dollars for information relative to Mullen and Jack."

Swegles met Mullen later that night. Mullen told his escape story, and Swegles invented one of his own. Mullen asked about Billy Brown. Swegles said he'd heard Brown was with friends in Indiana. He'd gotten rid of the team of horses and wagon, and could be trusted to keep quiet.

Mullen suggested they send a note to Hughes, letting him know it was safe to come back.

"What is the use?" Swegles objected. "You don't know but the officers may be on to us. There is nothing for Jack to do here, and there is no need of taking any chances."

As always, Swegles was playing it cool, working his role skillfully. Soon enough, he knew, Hughes would come back to his friends in Chicago.

Lanterns lit the floor and walls near the center of the labyrinth beneath the Lincoln Monument in Springfield. John Carroll Power, filthy and dripping sweat, stood in a shallow hole, tossing shovelfuls of wet dirt onto a growing pile. Beside the pile sat the big box holding Lincoln's coffin.

"I spent many hours and half hours digging," the custodian recalled. "When I would hear steps on the terrace overhead, I would extinguish lights, go out, give whatever attention might be required from visitors, and return to the work, for I had not then any assistant, and it would not do to trust a chance laborer I might have on the ground."

To tourists, everything at the monument appeared normal. They looked through the doors of the catacomb, and there was Lincoln's marble sarcophagus, intact and undamaged. They assumed Lincoln's body was in there. Power said nothing to correct them.

When the visitors left, Power went back to work on his secret hole. Then it started raining and water dripped through the stone terrace and into the labyrinth. Slowly, the hole filled with water. Power knew it could not be used. He piled a layer of lumber over Lincoln's box to hide it.

"I regarded this as only a temporary disposal of the matter," he said, "and fully expected to have further orders with reference to it in a short time."

No further orders came.

While it rained in Springfield, wet snow fell in Chicago. "Sick in bed all day," Tyrrell reported to Washington on November 12. But progress was being made. "Swegles seen Mullen last night, he is solid with Mullen. Jack Hughes is down at his father's. We shall work now to get them together, then arrest them soon as possible."

The next day's report to Chief Brooks was very short. "Louis Swegles did not call today, expected him all day," Tyrrell wrote from bed. "He is waiting for the arrival of Jack Hughes."

The wait continued. "My man Swegles has not appeared this day," wrote Tyrrell on the fourteenth. "I cannot get out yet being very sick."

November 15: "I cannot leave the house yet and no news from Swegles."

By November 16, nine days after the break-in, Tyrrell was done waiting. "Louis Swegles did not report this day to me," he noted. "I will start out myself tomorrow, my fever is all gone, feel better, but very weak."

As soon as Tyrrell got out of bed, his luck turned. When he dragged himself to Charles Deane's office on November

17, Swegles was there with news. Jack Hughes had just returned to Chicago. Tyrrell decided to arrest both Hughes and Mullen at the same time. Trying to nab them one at a time was no good—one might hear of the other getting pulled, and slip away.

While Swegles kept an eye on the Hub, Tyrrell brought in private eye John McGinn and a Chicago police detective named Denny Simmons to help with the final steps. Things started moving very quickly. At 8:00 that night, McGinn spotted Hughes on the street. At 8:40, Mullen showed up at the Hub, put on his apron, and began tending bar. At 10:30, Hughes entered the Hub.

"The time had arrived for action," reported Tyrrell.

Swegles walked away from the Hub, his work done. Tyrrell, McGinn, and Simmons gathered on the dark sidewalk outside the saloon. The detectives peered through the window and Tyrrell pointed out Hughes and Mullen. He'd have loved to make the bust himself, but he knew both coney men were armed. It was safer to send in men they had never seen before.

McGinn and Simmons opened the front door and walked in. Tyrrell watched through the window.

Jack Hughes appeared to be asleep. He was sprawled in a chair by the iron stove, eyes closed. Mullen was behind the bar.

McGinn walked past Hughes and stood between the dozing man and the back exit. Simmons went right to the bar.

Mullen smiled and asked the newcomers what they were drinking.

Two beers, Simmons said.

Mullen lifted a couple of glass mugs and headed down the bar to the tap. McGinn walked along with him. He waited until both of the bartender's hands were busy—one holding the mugs, the others pulling the tap handle. Then McGinn whipped out his pistol and stuck the barrel to Mullen's temple.

"Mullen, you are my man!"

Simmons raised his gun to Hughes's head. "Come along with me, my boy."

Hughes opened his eyes and looked up. "Who are you?"

"Never mind," said Simmons. "Get ready to go along with us."

Seeing both suspects with their hands in the air, Tyrrell charged into the saloon. He handcuffed the men together, led them out to a waiting police wagon, and climbed in to ride with them to Chicago's Central Police Station.

After watching the police lock Hughes and Mullen behind bars, Tyrrell telegraphed the good news to Chief Brooks in Washington. He arrived home at 1:00 A.M.

"Very weak and tired," he wrote, "but pleased by the results of the day."

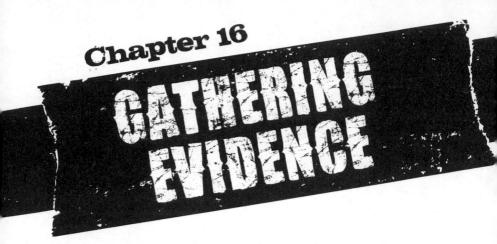

Chapter 16
GATHERING EVIDENCE

At 8:30 the next morning, Tyrrell was back at Central Station, with a new pair of shoes in his hand.

He walked through the station to the jail cells and handed the shoes, through the bars, to Jack Hughes. He told Hughes to put on this pair and hand out the ones he was wearing. Hughes's shoes were needed as evidence.

Hughes asked: Evidence of what?

Tyrrell explained that he and Mullen were being charged with attempting to rob Lincoln's tomb. The shoes placed Hughes in Springfield on the night of the crime. One of Tyrrell's private eyes had seen Hughes going into a shoemaker's shop, and the shoemaker could identify Hughes, as well as his own work on the man's shoes.

Both Hughes and Mullen assured Tyrrell they were

innocent. But before saying more, they wanted a lawyer. Specifically, they wanted William O'Brien, one of Chicago's top criminal defense lawyers.

O'Brien came to the prison later that day and met with his new clients in private. After the meeting, the lawyer announced his personal theory to the newspapers: Tyrrell and Elmer Washburn had designed an elaborate put-up job. They'd framed Hughes and Mullen in order to make a high-profile arrest and get themselves some good press.

O'Brien even invited a reporter from the *Chicago Times* to come down to the station to interview the poor victims, Hughes and Mullen. Tyrrell had no objection—he was curious to hear the bogus story O'Brien and his clients had concocted.

"The papers have implicated you in the attempted despoiling of Lincoln's tomb," the *Times* reporter said to Hughes and Mullen that night at the police station. "Now let me have your side of the story."

"I'll make a full statement," Hughes offered. "And I'll commence with the time I met this Swegles."

Tyrrell sat and listened as Hughes spun his tale. "Swegles, the horse thief," as Hughes called the roper, had started hanging around the Hub maybe a year before. He was always pitching ideas for crimes, Hughes explained, always bugging Hughes to come in on his latest scheme. For instance, he asked Hughes to help him pick up about $7,000 worth of stolen dry goods he'd stashed in an Indiana barn.

"I told him I wasn't that kind of a man," Hughes assured the reporter, "and I wouldn't go into the thing."

At about that time, Hughes said, he started noticing Patrick Tyrrell following him, and started hearing rumors that the Secret Service was working a put-up job on him.

Then, continued Hughes, right before the election, he and Mullen took a train to Springfield to visit Mullen's brother—Mullen had gotten a letter from a doctor saying his brother was very unwell. And there on the train was the incredibly annoying Swegles, greeting them with a grin and a bottle of whisky.

"We declined to take any, as we didn't want to be bothered by the fellow."

While Mullen looked for his brother, the horse thief tailed Hughes around Springfield, whispering something about a pile of money to be made in town.

"He then told me the whole particulars of the plan to rob Lincoln's grave of the body," Hughes explained.

"What did you say to that?" asked the reporter.

"I was never so astonished in my life. I told him it was out of my line of business and I wouldn't have anything to do with it."

And that's all there was to it, Hughes said. At 6:00 that evening, he and Mullen got back on the train. Unable to find Mullen's brother, they decided to visit Hughes's father at his farm. Then, ten days later in Chicago, they were arrested—for no reason.

"In my opinion," added Hughes, "the whole thing is a scheme to give Washburn and Tyrrell a little notoriety."

Hughes appeared cool and confident, noted the reporter. Mullen was the opposite, shifting nervously in his chair, avoiding eye contact.

The interview ended at 9:30. Tyrrell chained Hughes and Mullen together and took them to the train station. The overnight train carried the prisoners back to Springfield, to face charges in Lincoln's hometown.

Tyrrell must have been at least slightly concerned by Hughes's story. It was riddled with lies, but it sounded believable enough—it might even convince a jury.

On Monday morning, residents of Springfield crowded into the city jail to see the prisoners. Everyone was curious—what would men wicked enough to steal Lincoln's corpse look like? "Nearly all were disappointed," wrote one reporter. They looked like two ordinary guys.

Hughes and Mullen were officially charged with two crimes: "conspiracy to steal the remains of Abraham Lincoln" and "attempted larceny in trying to steal the casket . . . being the property of the Lincoln Monument Association." The combined charges carried a maximum sentence of up to five years in the state penitentiary. The judge set bail at $11,000 each—far more than Hughes and Mullen could raise. So they settled into prison to await trial.

Meanwhile, Tyrrell gathered evidence. He talked to John Carroll Power at the Lincoln Monument. Power assured

Tyrrell he had seen Hughes at the monument the afternoon of the break-in, and would testify to it in court. He talked to the ticket agents at the Springfield train station. The suspects claimed to have left on the 6:00 P.M. train, but no tickets had been sold to men meeting their description.

Then Thomas Keagle strolled into town. When the farmer read an account of the crime in the newspaper, he'd immediately thought of the two dust-covered travelers who'd come up to him while he was loading potatoes the morning after the election. So he came to take a look at the suspects and see if they were the same men.

Guards led Keagle into the city jail, but didn't point out any particular prisoners. There were eighteen small cells, holding a total of thirty-five men. The farmer walked down the hall between the cells, looking at faces. He stopped in front of cell number ten.

"Hello!" Keagle shouted to Hughes and Mullen. "Have they got you fellows here already?"

Mullen's face twisted into a bitter grin. Hughes sat straight-faced. Neither said a word.

Conductor John Foggett of the Illinois Central Railroad

also visited the jail. He identified Hughes and Mullen as the passengers who'd gotten on his train in Chestnut with a crazy story about buying cows and no money to pay their fare.

This was all decent evidence—it exposed lies in the story Hughes and Mullen had told. But none of it was conclusive. None of it proved that Hughes or Mullen were at the Lincoln Monument at the time of the break-in. The fact is, Tyrrell had botched the showdown at the monument. The whole case against the grave robbers rested on the testimony of Lewis Swegles, a known thief.

Hughes and Mullen were confident they'd soon be free. And they probably would have been—if only they could have sat tight.

But they were nervous about one thing: their lack of an alibi. If only someone would swear to having seen them far from Springfield while the monument break-in was occurring. The coney men worked out a plan. Mullen asked the prison guard for paper and a pencil.

His first letter was to fellow coney man Thomas Sharp—

the man who'd blown the first attempt to steal Lincoln's body earlier that year. Mullen asked Sharp to get a message to a mutual friend, Nathan "Lightning Rod" Curtis. Curtis was to tell police he'd seen Mullen and Hughes in Springfield on election day and invited them to stay over at his farm near town. Mullen wrote out the exact statement he wanted Curtis to make (the spelling is the coney man's own):

"Mullen and Hughes come to my house about 8 o'clock, that is the first time I ever scene Hughes. Mullen sayed they missed the train. We played cards a while, and they wanted to go, and I told them to stay all night. They stayed all night and had brackfast next morning. Lef about half past 6 o'clock in the morning."

Sharp got the letter, but he was sick of trouble with the law and decided not to deliver it to Curtis. Instead he brought it to the Springfield jail and handed it to a guard. The guard gave it to the sheriff, who gave it to Charles Reed, the lawyer leading the prosecution of Hughes and Mullen.

When Mullen didn't hear back from Sharp, he wrote a second letter, this time to a fellow coney man named

William Birdsall. Mullen asked Birdsall to tell police he'd seen Hughes and Mullen walking away from Springfield early in the evening on election day. He should say he gave the men a ride, and they stayed over at his house. "I think you can do it if only you use your head," Mullen urged his friend. "We will secure the money for you. I think we can raise you $35 cash."

This letter never even reached the post office. The jailer gave it directly to the prosecutor.

While in town, Tyrrell talked with the Springfield police chief, Abner Wilkinson. Wilkinson told Tyrrell about the rumors that had surfaced right before July 4—how members of the Logan County Gang were supposedly in town to steal Lincoln's body. Tyrrell contacted one of the gang, Vine Williams, and paid him ten bucks to answer a few questions. Williams confirmed that some of the Logan County boys— not him, of course—had planned to steal the casket, and that it had all been set up by Big Jim Kennally.

Tyrrell reported to his boss, "This establishes the fact beyond a doubt that the counterfeiters were active for some

way to liberate Ben Boyd, and Sir, the moving spirit was this same Jim Kennally, formerly of St. Louis."

It all fit. The Secret Service had no evidence against Big Jim, so he was safe for now—but at least Tyrrell knew the truth. Satisfied with his week's work in Springfield, he headed home to Chicago.

Back in his office, Tyrrell sat down to write a special report for Chief Brooks. He wanted an exact accounting of every penny spent on the Lincoln case. Tyrrell's report was long and detailed, listing each expense and its cost, including payments to Swegles and Billy Brown, train tickets, hotel rooms, hack rides, meals, telegraphs—even the two dollars Tyrrell spent on new shoes for Jack Hughes.

In total, Tyrrell reported, busting up the plot to steal Lincoln's body had cost the U.S. government $393.32.

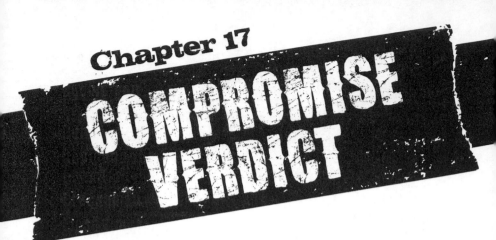

Chapter 17
COMPROMISE VERDICT

While Tyrrell got back to work in Chicago, the Hayes-Tilden war raged on. Tilden had definitely won about 250,000 more votes than Hayes—but even that was deceptive. In Southern states, bands of pro-Democratic thugs had openly used violence and intimidation to prevent thousands of African American men from voting. Republican-controlled election boards in the South struck back by throwing out thousands of valid Democratic votes. So basically, there was no way to figure out whom voters had actually meant to elect.

As 1877 began, both sides were still battling over the three undecided states: Florida, South Carolina, and Louisiana. The inauguration of the new president was set for March 5.

"Tilden or blood!" shouted furious Democratic crowds.

There was talk of armed marches on Washington—maybe even another Civil War.

A panicked Congress scrambled to set up a special commission made up of five members of the House of Representatives, five members of the Senate, and five Supreme Court justices. Their task was to decide who won the election. The commission had eight Republicans and seven Democrats.

The vote was 8–7 for the Republican, Rutherford B. Hayes.

The trial of Jack Hughes and Terrence Mullen began on May 29, 1877. The Springfield courtroom, said a local reporter, was "crowded to the utmost capacity."

The prosecutor, Charles Reed, produced a parade of witnesses. The manager of the St. Charles House identified Hughes and Mullen as guests in his hotel on election day, showing the jury the register book in which the two men had signed in—under false names. Charles Elkin, the streetcar conductor, testified that he saw two men running from the Lincoln Monument grounds late that night. The farmers

Thomas Keagle and John Dixon told of seeing Hughes and Mullen the next morning.

John Carroll Power testified about seeing Hughes and Swegles at the monument the afternoon of the robbery attempt. Private eye George Hay told the jury about his embarrassing accidental gunshot, and identified Hughes as one of the men he'd seen at the monument while waiting inside Memorial Hall. Tyrrell produced the tools left behind by the grave robbers, and told his story. Swegles spent two hours on the stand, detailing his work as a roper and his role in the plot. Defense attorneys attacked the roper, calling him a liar and a thief, but Swegles "was not shaken in the least," reported the *Illinois State Journal*.

This was all very damaging to the defendants, but it was the two letters Mullen wrote from jail that really sank them. Charles Reed showed them to the jury and had them read aloud. Here was Mullen, in his own words, begging friends to provide him and Hughes with bogus alibis.

When it was Hughes's turn to take the stand, he stuck to the same basic story he'd been telling since the arrest. Sure, he and Mullen had been in Springfield on election day—to find Mullen's sick brother. Sure, they'd been seen with Swegles—because he kept following them around, urging them to rob the Lincoln Monument. In fact, Hughes explained, that's why they left town in such a hurry that night. They knew Swegles was about to commit this crazy crime, and they knew they'd been seen in town with him. So they hit the road, to avoid unjust suspicion.

Mullen's version was the same, but delivered without Hughes's brash confidence. He talked so quietly the judge had to keep asking him to speak up.

Closing statements finished up at 1:00 A.M. The jury met all night, quickly agreeing that the men were guilty. But there was debate over the proper punishment, which could be up to five years. Hughes and Mullen did not impress the jury as particularly bright—they just didn't seem capable of designing a complex plot to steal and ransom Lincoln's body. Several jurors were convinced Swegles was really the brains of the operation.

The next morning at 9:00 A.M., the courtroom was packed again to hear the jury read its verdict: "We the jury find the defendants guilty as charged in the indictment, and fix the term of their confinement in the penitentiary at one year each."

Tyrrell was disappointed. "The sentence, one year in the penitentiary, is a compromise verdict," he complained to Chief Brooks.

Discussing the surprisingly light sentence, the *Chicago Times* expressed the same doubts as the jurors. "There is reason to believe that the actual extent of the plot is not yet exposed, and many think that Mullen and Hughes, though really guilty of complicity in the plot, did not contrive it, but are really the tools of smarter men."

That reporter had no idea how right he was.

Hughes and Mullen were handcuffed again and taken by train to Joliet. There they joined Ben Boyd as prisoners at the Illinois State Penitentiary.

Tyrrell returned to Chicago and went back to chasing coney men. On June 21, he took a quick break to visit Robert Lincoln, who'd asked him to stop by. When Tyrrell arrived, Lincoln pointed out a large portrait of his father—he wanted Tyrrell to have the painting as a gift for protecting his father's remains. "I thanked Mr. Lincoln for his kind appreciation of my actions, and said that I had only done my duty."

There was just one last detail to settle. "Chief, I have the tools captured by me on the night of November 7, 1876, in the Monument, which were used as evidence in the trial of Terrence Mullen and Jack Hughes, what shall I do with them?"

Tyrrell suggested the Lincoln Monument Association might want them. Brooks agreed. That summer, Tyrrell traveled to Springfield to investigate one of his ongoing counterfeiting cases. Before leaving town, he rode out to the Lincoln Monument and handed John Carroll Power a box containing a hammer, a file, a bull's-eye lantern, a pair of pliers, a saw blade, and a broken padlock.

Power put it all on display in his glass cases in Memorial Hall.

FINAL RESTING PLACE?

Six months later, John Carroll Power was still waiting for directions from his bosses about what to do with Lincoln's coffin. It was still sitting there on the damp labyrinth floor.

In the summer of 1877, workers came to renovate one of the monument's walls. That meant going into the labyrinth, and Power realized that workmen would certainly notice the coffin. Instead of having them stumble upon it, he decided to tell them it was there—and who was in it.

Less than two days later, Power overheard people in Springfield swapping the latest rumor: Lincoln's body was sitting in the dirt under a stack of rotting lumber.

Horrified, Power rushed to John Stuart of the Monument Association to discuss the crisis. Stuart was no help. He and the other elderly association members just couldn't face going back into that suffocating space and hauling that heavy coffin again—especially not in summer.

All Power could do was hope the rumors would die down.

Patrick Tyrrell traveled to Joliet on May 22, 1878—the day Jack Hughes and Terrence Mullen were due to get out of prison.

While at the state pen, Tyrrell stopped in to see Ben Boyd. In the two and a half years since Boyd's arrest, he and Tyrrell had become friendly. Boyd even offered his former nemesis occasional advice on catching coney men.

Tyrrell then waited outside the main door of the prison. At 1:00 P.M., Hughes walked out a free man—or so he thought. But Tyrrell grabbed his arm and slapped handcuffs on his wrists.

"I informed Jack that there was another case against him," Tyrrell reported, "that he would have to come to Chicago."

Hughes was still facing charges for passing fake

money—remember, he'd been a wanted man even before the Lincoln job disaster. Now Tyrrell hauled him to Chicago, and a judge sent him right back to the Illinois State Penitentiary, this time for three years of hard labor.

Mullen, meanwhile, returned to Chicago only to find that while he was in jail, Big Jim Kennally had sold the Hub and disappeared with the money.

Shortly after midnight on November 7, 1878, a gang of body snatchers snuck into a gated cemetery in New York City and pried up the stone slab above the burial vault of a wealthy merchant named Alexander Stewart. The men climbed down into the vault, cracked open Stewart's casket, shoved the rotting body into a bag, and hurried off.

The gang contacted Stewart's family and demanded a $250,000 ransom for the dead man's remains. The story was huge news around the country, and soon showed up in the Springfield papers—reminding everyone of the attempt to steal Lincoln.

"It appeared to me," Power recalled, "as though half the people of Springfield accosted me on the street, or came to the Monument and inquired if the body of Lincoln was safe. I did not think it was, but evaded their questions as well as I could."

Again, Powers begged members of the Monument Association for help. Again, they said they were too old, the casket was too heavy, it was too hot down there. . . .

Power was done waiting. Acting on his own, he recruited five trustworthy young men. When they met him at the monument on the night of November 18, Power handed out shovels and lanterns, and led the way through Monument Hall into the labyrinth. They dug a hole and placed Lincoln's coffin at the bottom.

Three nights later, Power was finally beginning to relax when he got another shock. He was home after work, going through his mail, and came to a strange postcard. The short message read:

"Be careful. Do not be alone, particularly Thursday night, Nov. 21st"

The note was signed only with the letter "C." It had been sent from Chicago.

Panic swept over Power again. It *was* the night of

November 21! He thought about rushing back to the monument, but it was late, and he was scared to go alone. "Little sleep came to my eyes that night," he said.

Early next morning he hurried into the labyrinth. There were no footsteps, no signs anyone had tried to break in. "All was safe," he reported.

Who sent the postcard? What did it mean? Power never found out—and the mystery haunted him. "Is there real danger?" he wondered. "Is there another scheme to capture the remains of Lincoln? Or is someone trying to play a joke?"

Unable to face this fear alone, Power talked to the men who had helped him bury Lincoln's coffin. Together they agreed to form a secret organization with just one mission: protect Lincoln's body. They called themselves the Lincoln Guard of Honor.

"We were never bound by any oath," Power said of the Guard, "but something much stronger—our own sense of honor."

In March 1880, Terrence Mullen was arrested for passing counterfeit bills in St. Louis. Tyrrell rushed to the jail, eager

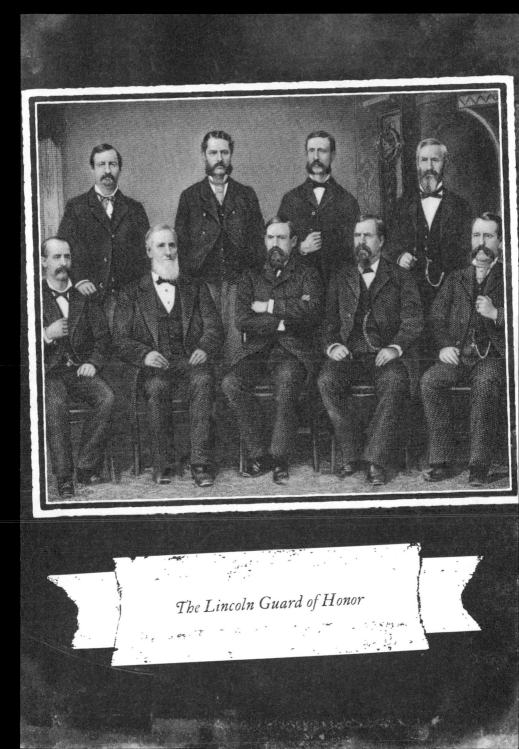

The Lincoln Guard of Honor

to talk with the coney man. Just as he'd hoped, Mullen was furious with Big Jim Kennally, and agreed to talk. Acting on Mullen's information, Secret Service agents caught Kennally with a stash of bogus $10 bills in his possession. A judge gave him two years in prison.

Lewis Swegles may have helped save Lincoln's body, but he just couldn't stay clean. In one of his daily reports from 1880, Tyrrell mentioned that Swegles was back behind bars, doing twelve years in Joliet for burglary.

What about Boyd's brother-in-law, Pete McCartney, the coney man who prided himself on wriggling out of any trap? His luck ran out, too. McCartney was nabbed in Indiana shoving fake twenties. He tried to bribe the cops with $1,500 in real money, but they hauled him off to jail. At trial, McCartney promised to change his ways, but the judge wasn't buying it.

"There is little hope for reform," the judge told McCartney. "It is my duty to sentence you to fifteen years at hard labor in the State Prison."

This time, McCartney served every day of his sentence.

Mary Lincoln died on July 16, 1882. Her coffin was placed in the catacomb at the Lincoln Monument—next to the marble sarcophagus that everyone assumed held Abraham Lincoln's remains.

Robert Lincoln knew the box was empty, and knew his mother wanted to be buried beside her husband. So late one night, Power and the other members of the Lincoln Guard of Honor carried Mary into the labyrinth, dug a hole, and set her down next to Abe.

"I cannot adequately thank you," Robert wrote to the Guard. "I think it will be best that no change should be made for a long time to come."

But the story wasn't over.

The rumors never faded—people continued whispering that Lincoln wasn't actually in his marble sarcophagus. Almost every day, Power faced the same question from tourists: Was the body in the box or wasn't it?

"We put it back there the second day after the attempt to steal it," Power always said. And that was strictly true; he just didn't mention that they'd taken it back out again.

When people pestered him for details, Powers would say: "I suppose you wish to know if there is not further danger, if so, I can assure you that it is absolutely safe."

If they asked more questions about the body, Power cut them off.

And that was the end of the discussion. Power refused to say more. He insisted that the body was safe—and he knew in his heart it wasn't. Nothing but door locks and a few inches of dirt stood between Lincoln and a new team of body snatchers.

After several more years of pleading with the Monument Association, Power finally convinced the members it was time for a permanent solution. Workers pulled up the tiles of the catacomb floor and dug a deep hole. On the morning of April 14, 1887, members of the Monument Association and Guard of Honor gathered at the monument. A Springfield plumber named Leon Hopkins was there too, though he didn't know why he'd been asked to come.

"I guess we might as well go to work," Power said.

The men carried the two bodies out of the labyrinth

and set them down in Memorial Hall. Before they placed the coffins in the new hole, there was one last piece of business—crazy rumors about the true whereabouts of Lincoln's remains had to be put to rest once and for all.

"After so many changes," Power explained, "it was indispensably necessary to identify the body of the President."

The lid of Lincoln's wooden coffin was lifted. Then Leon Hopkins found out why he was there—he was called forward and told to carefully cut open the inner lead coffin. Hopkins did this, gently bending back a flap of the soft metal above Lincoln's head.

Sunlight slanted through the open door into the coffin. Everyone pushed forward to look.

"Of the eighteen or nineteen persons present, nearly all had personally seen the President in life," Power reported. "There was not one who expressed the slightest doubt that he was looking at the features of the beloved President."

"The remains were somewhat shrunken," added the Monument Association members in a signed statement, "but the features were quite natural, and we could readily recognize them as the features of the former illustrious President of our Nation, and our former friend and fellow citizen."

Hopkins then bent the lead back into place, and soldered the seams to make them airtight. The two coffins were carried around the monument to the catacomb and lowered into the new hole. Then workers poured in four feet of concrete, and when it hardened, laid the marble tiles back down just as they had been before.

A very relieved Power could finally report that Lincoln's body was safe.

After serving his ten years, Ben Boyd was released from prison and went back to work as an engraver—this time, doing perfectly legal work at a factory. "He has 'squared it,'" reported the *Chicago Tribune*. "He is a living personification of what a man can do if he will to regain a footing in society and make an honest living." Secret Service Chief James Brooks was impressed. "Boyd took his medicine manfully, and never whimpered."

John Carroll Power stayed on as custodian at the Lincoln

Lincoln's coffin being hoisted
out of the ground

Monument. In his spare time, he wrote *History of an Attempt to Steal the Body of Abraham Lincoln*, the first book about this story, and the only one by an eyewitness. He died in 1894, at age 74, and was buried in Oak Ridge Cemetery, very close to the monument he guarded for twenty years.

Patrick Tyrrell served in the Secret Service until his retirement in 1899. Nothing is known about how he spent the next twenty-one years, but he lived until 1920. He died at age 89, and was buried in Chicago.

Incredibly, Abraham Lincoln's body was not done moving.

By 1900, the poorly built Lincoln Monument was starting to collapse. Before the foundation could be rebuilt, the bodies of Lincoln and his family had to be safely removed.

Workers first carried out the coffins of Lincoln's three sons. Then they cracked through the concrete above Abraham's and Mary's coffins. All five bodies were locked in a temporary vault near the monument until the renovations were complete.

In April 1901, they were returned to the catacomb. Mary and the boys were sealed in crypts in the catacomb

The five Lincoln family coffins being reburied in 1901

wall. Abraham was placed back into the white marble sarcophagus that had held his body at the time of the robbery.

Robert Lincoln came to take a look. He couldn't believe his eyes. After everything that had happened, his father's body was sitting there, aboveground, exactly where it had been in 1876!

He ordered a new hole dug in the catacomb. He wanted it ten feet deep, and he wanted a steel cage set inside.

On September 26, 1901, surviving members of the Guard of Honor gathered to move Lincoln's casket one last time. As soon as they got there, the men began to argue—should they have one last look in the coffin, just to make *absolutely* sure Lincoln was still in there? Robert had specifically told them not to open the casket. They decided to anyway.

Once again, they sent for Leon Hopkins, the plumber.

An Honor Guard member named Joseph Lindley also telephoned the school of his thirteen-year-old son, Fleetwood, and talked with Fleetwood's teacher. The teacher told Fleetwood to race out to the Lincoln Monument right away. The boy wasn't sure what the hurry was, but he hopped on his bicycle, sped to the monument, peddled up to Memorial

Fleetwood Lindley

Hall, pushed his bike inside, and leaned it against the wall.

Someone shut the door behind Fleetwood. The room darkened. A single electric lamp threw a pool of light on a casket, which rested on two sawhorses. People stopped talking as Leon Hopkins stepped forward with a blowtorch. He began cutting open the lead, just as he had done fourteen years before.

Fleetwood crowded in for a closer look. He had only seen Lincoln in photographs, but when the casket was opened, he recognized the famous man immediately. "His face was chalky white," Fleetwood would never forget. "His clothes were mildewed."

"He looked just like a statue of himself lying there," said another witness.

Everyone agreed: This was Abraham Lincoln. Hopkins pushed the lead flap back into place.

"I watched the shadow of the lid fall across Lincoln's face," recalled Guard of Honor member B. H. Monroe. "That face disappeared from mortal view forever."

Fleetwood lifted one of the leather straps attached to the coffin, and helped lower Lincoln's body into the steel cage sitting inside the ten-foot hole in the catacomb floor. The cage was locked and workers then began pouring in tons of wet concrete. As the concrete slowly dried, the body of Abraham Lincoln was sealed inside a massive, rock-hard block.

It's still there.

BODY SNATCHER BONUS SECTION

We'll never know what body-snatching stories Swegles told Mullen and Hughes during their meeting at the Hub described on page 85. But given his criminal past and shady friends, Swegles may well have known of some of the more famous "ghouls" of the Midwest. Actually, body snatchers didn't like to be called ghouls. They preferred to be known as resurrectionists.

Swegles may have spoken fondly of the notorious William Cunningham, who worked the bone orchards in and around Cincinnati. Cunningham was a wagon driver by day. At night, he dug up dead people.

He had the whole thing down to a science. First he dug a small hole—just two feet by two—right above the coffin. He broke open the box and slid hooks under the fresh corpse's arms. Using ropes and brute force, he then hauled the body out of its box and up to the surface.

Cunningham stripped off the stiff's fancy burial outfit and dressed it in well-worn, everyday clothes. Then he sat the cold body next to him in his wagon, and drove from the cemetery toward one of the city's medical colleges.

A doctor who occasionally bought bodies from Cunningham recalled seeing the body snatcher returning from one of these late-night trips. "There was a corpse sitting in the buggy on the seat beside him," the doctor said. "The corpse was dressed up in an old coat, vest, and hat. Cunny held the reins in his right hand while he steadied the corpse with his left arm around the waist of his silent companion."

It didn't look quite right, Cunningham knew. So whenever someone walked by on the street, Cunningham turned angrily to his passenger and slapped him on the cheek.

"Sit up!" he shouted. "This is the last time I'm going to take you home when you get drunk. The idea of a man with a family disgracing himself this way!"

Cunningham was shot a couple of times by angry

relatives of the dead, but that didn't slow him down much. He dug up and sold so many corpses, he became known as the "Prince of the Ghouls." Shortly before his own death in 1871, Cunningham sold his own body to the Medical College of Ohio—for five dollars.

Then there was Dr. Joseph Nash McDowell, one of the most respected experts on human anatomy in the Midwest. When McDowell wanted a body, he cut out the middleman—instead of paying a resurrectionist, he recruited a few medical students and they did the job themselves.

One day McDowell learned about an especially interesting corpse, that of a girl who'd just died of a rare disease. Desperate to dissect and study the body, the doctor and two students dug it up and snuck it back to their school. But the girl's family immediately discovered the theft. A bunch of them grabbed guns and headed for McDowell's lab.

McDowell was determined not to lose that corpse. He sprinted into his dark dissecting room with a lantern in his hand, lifted the light body with his other hand, and headed for the stairs.

"I had ascended one flight of stairs when out went my lamp," McDowell recalled. "I laid down the corpse and re-struck a light. I then picked up the body, when out went my light again. I felt for another match in my pocket."

Finally stashing the body in the attic, the doctor raced down the dark stairs. As he passed a window, he heard two men talking on the street below. "One had a shotgun," he remembered, "the other a revolver."

Just as McDowell reached the door of his dissecting room, someone lit a lantern at the bottom of the stairwell. Five or six armed men started up the stairs. McDowell darted into the room and shut the door.

There were several operating tables in the room. On most were corpses, covered with sheets.

As heavy footsteps pounded the stairs, McDowell dove onto the table that had held the young girl's body only minutes before. He pulled the sheet over his face and tried not to breathe.

The men came in with guns and lanterns. "They uncovered one body—it was that of a man," McDowell said. "Then they came to two women with black hair—the girl they were looking for had flaxen hair."

Then one of the men pulled back the sheet over Dr. McDowell.

"Here's a fellow who died in his boots. I guess he's a fresh one."

The doctor lay like stone.

The man dropped the sheet back over his head. Moments later, the searchers left the room and hurried back down the stairs. McDowell waited until the coast was clear, then sprinted out a back door. He returned to the college the next morning and retrieved his prize from the attic.

"We dissected the body," he said, "buried the fragments, and had no further trouble."

Body snatching was dangerous business, but many doctors were willing to accept the risk—for just the right specimen.

"I was one of four who had agreed to exhume the body of a man of immense size," a doctor named Marmaduke Burr Wright recalled of one of his many memorable visits to the graveyards of Cincinnati. With picks, shovels, rope, and a large sack concealed under long coats, the men walked down dark roads to a cemetery behind a small church. Crouching in the building's black shadows, they looked out at the graves. There was a problem. Lantern light still streamed from the windows of surrounding houses. The light bounced off the stone graves, giving the bone orchard an eerie gray glow.

The men wrapped their jackets around themselves and waited. Over the next few hours, one by one, the lanterns went out. Then Dr. Wright's team got to work.

One man guarded the front gate to the cemetery, another stood near the back. Wright and the fourth man started shoveling up the loose soil of a fresh grave. They quickly dug down to the top of a wooden coffin. Wright jumped into the hole, brushed away the dirt, and inspected the box. Thick wood, he saw, held together with quality screws. He slid one end of a pick under the lid, and started working the handle back with quick jerks.

The coffin lid bent and creaked and—*CRACK!*

Wright froze.

The sound of snapping wood seemed to bounce like thunder from house to house. Dogs started barking. Lights appeared in windows. Dim figures could be seen in the windows, peering out. A very long minute passed.

"Not a footstep, however, was heard approaching us," Wright remembered. "We returned to our labor."

The doctor looped a rope around the dead man's chest and climbed out of the hole. He and the others heaved, backing up as they pulled, until the big body flopped up onto the grass. Two men slipped a sack over the corpse while the others gathered up the tools. Then the team hoisted the dead man onto their shoulders and left the cemetery.

"We had not gone far with our burden," recalled Wright, "when, as we turned a corner, a man came suddenly upon us."

The stranger came toward them, staggering and muttering. He was so drunk he passed by without seeing a thing.

A bit farther down the road, Wright and the crew spotted an old wheelbarrow by a shed. They dumped their load into it. The cart's rusty axle groaned and squeaked under the weight, but at least they could move faster. The men hurried toward their lab, where they could hide the body.

"Every step we took was attended with hazard," Wright said of the trip home. The sky was already lightening to a faint yellow. Smoke began rising from the chimneys of farmhouses along the road. The butcher drove past in his wagon.

The group was in sight of their building when a man turned a corner, stopped, and blocked their path.

"Doctors, what have you there?" he demanded.

Wright and the others let go of the wheelbarrow and stepped back.

The man looked over the strangely shaped sack. He opened the top a little and peered in. Confused, he reached in his hand and felt around—and touched the cold flesh of a dead human face.

The man shuddered, pulled out his hand, raised his arms high in the air, and ran screaming down the streets of Cincinnati.

"We seized this as the only favorable moment of escape," said Wright. Pushing the squeaking wheelbarrow through town, they reached Wright's lab, raced in, and locked the door behind them.

Scenes like this continued until the late 1800s, when states began passing laws making it easier for doctors to legally acquire the bodies they needed for their studies. This destroyed the demand for stolen corpses, putting the ghouls out of business.

GLOSSARY OF PHRASES

Body snatchers — criminals who dug up bodies and sold them, usually to medical colleges

Bogus — phony; counterfeit money

Bone orchard — graveyard

Boodle carrier — criminal, usually a teenager, who carried counterfeit money for a shover

Boodle game — technique used by counterfeiters to spend fake money without being caught

Coney — counterfeit currency

Confound the fellow — expression of anger, frustration toward another

Cracksman — skilled safecracker

Flush times — good times, making easy money

Ghouls — body snatchers

Hack — hired wagon; similar to a taxi today

Lay — course of action; criminal plan

Out of joint — messed-up, gone wrong

Pipe — follow secretly

Pull — arrest

Put-up job — to frame, falsely accuse someone of a crime

Roper — undercover informant for police

Row — fight

Shootin` iron — pistol

Shover — criminal who passes counterfeit money in stores and banks

Toes up — dead

SOURCE NOTES

The two absolutely essential primary sources behind this book are Secret Service Agent Patrick Tyrrell's handwritten daily reports and Lincoln Monument custodian John Carroll Power's *History of an Attempt to Steal the Body of Abraham Lincoln*. Newspaper articles from the time of the crime, a few of which include interviews with Lewis Swegles, Jack Hughes, and other participants, also added key eyewitness details and quotes. Here's a list of all the sources I used while researching this book.

Bowen, Walter, and Harry Edward Neal. *The United States Secret Service*. Philadelphia: Chilton Company, 1960.

Burnham, George. *Three Years with Counterfeiters, Smugglers, and Boodle Carriers*. Boston: Jackson, Dale & Co., 1875.

Campbell, Polly. "The Body Snatchers: Medical students needed corpses to dissect, which spawned a new profession." Cincinnati, January 1989, pp. 29–31.

Chicago Daily Tribune. "Ben Boyd and Wife." June 20, 1876.

———. "At the Custom House." June 21, 1876.

———. "Today." Nov. 7, 1876.

———. "Dastardly Attempt to Despoil the Lincoln Monument." Nov. 8, 1876.

———. "After the Surprise." Nov. 18, 1876.

———. "At the Tomb." Nov. 18, 1876.

———. "The Arrest." Nov. 18, 1876.

———. "The Hub." Nov. 18, 1876.

———. "The Plot" Nov. 18, 1876.

———. "The Scheme Unfolded." Nov. 18, 1876.

———. "Tyrrell at Springfield." Nov. 18, 1876.

———. "Ben Boyd and the Counterfeit Business." Nov. 18, 1876.

———. "Lincolns Remains." Nov. 19, 1876.

———. "Bail Set." Nov. 21, 1876

———. "Criminal News." Nov. 23, 1876.

———. "The Vandals." Dec. 9, 1876

———. "The Counterfeiters." May 3, 1882.

———. "Bad Men." May 21, 1883.

———. "The King of Counterfeiters." Nov. 12, 1884.

———. "They Pass Bogus Money." Aug. 11, 1889.

———. "Death Notices: Patrick D. Tyrrell." Apr. 5, 1920.

Chicago Times. "The Local Field." Nov. 7, 1876.

———. "Ghoulish Game: Bagged by Washburn and Detectives." Nov. 18, 1876.

———. "The Body-Snatchers." Nov. 19, 1876.

———. "The Trial of Mullen and Hughes at Springfield." May 30, 31, 1877.

Craughwell, Thomas J. *Stealing Lincoln's Body.* Cambridge, MA: Harvard University Press, 2007.

Glaser, Lynn. *Counterfeiting in America.* New York: Clarkson N. Potter, 1968.

Fulton (IL) Journal. "Ben Boyd, Counterfeiter, Nabbed at Last." Oct. 29, 1875.

———. "The Counterfeiters." Nov. 5, 1875.

Illinois Daily State Journal (Springfield). "The Elections." Nov. 8, 1876.

———. "Lincoln's Tomb: The Arrest of the Violators of his Sepulchre." Nov. 20, 1876.

———. "News from Springfield" Nov. 23, 1876.

———. "Lincoln Tomb Robbers." June 1, 1877.

Illinois Daily State Register (Springfield). "Tilden is the Man." Nov. 8, 1876.

———. "Criminal News." Nov. 22, 1876.

———. "Trial and Conviction of Mullen and Hughes." May 31, 1877.

Johnson, David. *Illegal Tender: Counterfeiting and the Secret Service in Nineteenth Century America.* Washington, DC: Smithsonian Institution Press, 1995.

Juettner, Otto. *Daniel Drake and His Followers; Historical and Biographical Sketches.* Cincinnati: Harvey Publishing Company, 1909.

Kunhardt, Philip, Peter Kunhardt & Peter Kunhardt, Jr. *Looking for Lincoln: The Making of an American Icon.* New York: Alfred A. Knopf, 2008.

Kunhardt, Dorothy Meserve. "The Incredible Story of What Happened to Lincoln's Body." *Life*, February 15, 1963, pp. 83–88.

Kunhardt, Dorothy Meserve, and Philip B. Kunhardt Jr. *Twenty Days: A Narrative in Pictures of the Assassination of Abraham Lincoln and the Twenty Days and Nights that Followed.* New York: Harper and Row, 1965.

Lachman, Charles. *The Last Lincolns: The Rise and Fall of a Great American Family.* New York: Sterling Publishing Co., Inc., 2008.

Lewis, Lloyd. *Myths After Lincoln.* New York: Grosset & Dunlap, 1957.

Melanson, Phillip. *The Secret Service: The Hidden History of an Enigmatic Agency.* New York: Carroll & Graf Publishers, 2002.

Morris, Ray Jr. *Fraud of the Century: Rutherford B. Hayes, Samuel Tilden, and the Stolen Election of 1876.* New York: Simon & Schuster, 2003.

National Lincoln Monument Association, Report of the Custodian, 1876–1878. Abraham Lincoln Presidential Library, Springfield, IL.

New York Times. "An Old Counterfeiter Arrested." Oct. 23, 1875.

———. "Peter McCartney Imprisoned." Dec. 2, 1876.

———. "A Remarkable Counterfeit." Oct. 1, 1877.

———. "Ghouls in New York City." Nov. 8, 1878.

Power, John Carroll. *Abraham Lincoln: His Life, Public Services, Death, and Great Funeral Cortege.* Chicago and Springfield, IL: H. W. Printing and Publishing House, 1889.

———. *History of an Attempt to Steal the Body of Abraham Lincoln.* Chicago and Springfield, IL: H.W. Rokker Printing and Publishing House, 1890.

Records of the United States Secret Service, Daily Reports of Patrick D. Tyrrell, 1875–1878. National Archives, College Park, MD.

Rehnquist, William. *Centennial Crisis: The Disputed Election of 1876.* New York: Vintage Books, 2005.

Scott, Kenneth. *Counterfeiting in Colonial America.* New York: Oxford University Press, 1957.

Shultz, Suzanne, M. *Body Snatching: The Robbing of Graves for the Education of Physicians in Early Nineteenth Century America.* Jefferson, NC: McFarland & Company, 1992.

Speer, Bonnie Stahlman. *The Great Abraham Lincoln Hijack: 1876 Attempt to Steal Body of President Lincoln.* Norman, OK: Reliance Press, 1990.

INDEX

ACKNOWLEDGEMENTS

This is a mighty strange story, and I had a lot to learn before I could even hope to do it justice. Thanks to Thomas Craughwell, author of *Stealing Lincoln's Body*, for sharing his extensive knowledge of this bizarre tale, and for offering some great suggestions of places to find even more information. And thanks to the National Archives for making it easy to get digital reproductions of Patrick Tyrrell's daily reports. Without access to these records, this story could not be told.

When I traveled to Springfield to study the scene of the crime, Dr. James Cornelius, curator of the Abraham Lincoln Library, took the time to answer questions and help me find some obscure but priceless sources. He even led me to a storage room, opened a drawer—and there were the tools Hughes and Mullen used to bust into Lincoln's tomb!

Next I went to the Lincoln Monument, where staff member Mikle Siere showed me around the grounds and let me see stuff most tourists never get to see—like the old dirt-floor labyrinth under the monument where Tyrrell waited, gun in hand, for the robbery to begin.

A special thanks to Brenda Murray at Scholastic for giving me the chance to write this book and for her excellent edits along the way, and thanks to Ken Wright for helping to steer this project my way. And as usual, thanks to Rachel, always my first reader.